Ernesto 'Che' Guevara's

The Motorcycle Diaries

Study notes for Area of Study:
Discovery
2015-2018 HSC

Renee Carr

Five Senses Education Pty Ltd
2/195 Prospect Highway
Seven Hills 2147
New South Wales
Australia

First Published 2014

Carr, Renee
Top Notes – The Motorcycle Diaries
ISBN 978 -1- 74130 – 993 – 5

CONTENTS

TOP NOTES SERIES

This series has been created to assist HSC students of English in their understanding of set texts. Top Notes are easy to read, provide analysis of issues and discuss important ideas contained in the texts.

Particular care has been taken to ensure that students are able to examine each text in the context of the module it has been allocated to or the Area of Study, Discovery.

Each text generally includes:

- Notes on the specific module
- Plot summary
- Character analysis
- Setting
- Thematic concerns
- Language studies
- Essay questions and a modelled response
- Other textual material
- Study practice questions
- Useful quotes

We have covered the areas we feel are important for students in their study of texts. I am sure you will find these Top Notes useful in your studies of English.

Bruce Pattinson
Series Editor

AREA OF STUDY: DISCOVERY

'We learn wisdom from failure much more than from success. We often discover what will do, by finding out what will not do; and probably he who never made a mistake never made a discovery.'

SAMUEL SMILES

The Area of Study set for the 2015–18 HSC is *Discovery*. It is compulsory to study this topic as prescribed by the Board of Studies. Remember you are supposed to analyse your texts with reference to varying aspects of *Discovery*. Markers will be looking to see evidence of deep conceptual understanding of the Area of Study and you are encouraged to support your views with close textual referencing.

In the Area of Study you will be analysing many texts that are related to the idea of discovery. You will analyse texts not only to investigate the ideas they present about this area but also how they deliver these ideas. This means you will be looking closely at the techniques composers use to represent ideas and shape meaning. You will also be looking at relationships between texts. Overall, you will become an expert on discovery- the different notions people have about it and the various ways composers manipulate techniques to communicate their ideas about the topic. The material in this Top Note will help you do that.

Specifically you will look at:

- A set text from the following list of fourteen texts. **You will only study one of these.**
  - *Wrack* – James Bradley
  - *The Awakening* – Kate Chopin
  - *A Short History of Nearly Everything* – Bill Bryson
  - *The Motorcycle Diaries* – Ernesto 'Che' Guevara
  - *Swallow the Air* – Tara June Winch
  - *Away* – Michael Gow
  - *Rainbow's End* – Jane Harrison
  - *Frank Hurley - The Man Who Made History* – Simon Nasht
  - *Life of Pi* – Ang Lee
  - *The Tempest* – William Shakespeare
  - *Selected Poems* – Robert Gray
  - *Selected Poems* – Rosemary Dobson
  - *Selected Poems* – Robert Frost
  - *Go Back To Where You Came From* – selected episodes – Ivan O'Mahoney
- Additional related texts of your own choosing.

You must write about your set text and additional texts of your own choosing in the first English paper of the HSC examination.

> *I hope that posterity will judge me kindly, not only as to the things which I have explained, but also to those which I have intentionally omitted so as to leave to others the pleasure of discovery.*
>
> **RENE DESCARTES**

WHAT DOES THE BOARD OF STUDIES REQUIRE FOR THE AREA OF STUDY?

The Board of Studies documentation says of the Area of Study: Discovery that it;

> *'requires students to explore the ways in which the concept of discovery is represented in and through texts.' (p 9)*

The document English Stage 6 Prescriptions: Area of Study Electives and Texts (August 2013) notes that perceptions of discovery can encompass many things and are shaped by context.

- Students can consider –not only discovery but also rediscovery.
- That discovery may be planned or unplanned and may lead to new worlds and values.
- Discoveries can question and challenge and lead to different conclusions.

You will also need to consider that the 'process of discovering can vary according to personal, cultural, historical and social contexts and values.'

Below is an abbreviated version of what the Board requires of students.

'In their responses and compositions students examine, question, reflect and speculate on':

- their own experiences of discovery, personally and through texts.

- the assumptions underlying the representations of discovery.
- the effects of composers' choices of techniques.
- the ways in which the study of discovery has helped them understand the world and themselves.

Think carefully about the wording that is used so that you can adopt this language for your own work.

If this is what is required by the Board of Studies you need to examine the concept of discovery carefully so you can respond adequately. We would recommend that you read the complete document which is on the Board of Studies website (http://www.bostes.nsw.edu.au) and can be downloaded in Word or PDF formats.

UNDERSTANDING THE AREA OF STUDY

'There is no better high than discovery'

- E. O. WILSON

Discovery is often associated with adventure. The word *Discovery* conjures childhood dreams of exotic locations, intrepid explorers in jungles discovering lost tribes and great treasures. Movies embrace this theme. The Discovery Channel exists to help people to discover facts vicariously. The concept behind the never-ending Star Trek series is to 'explore strange new worlds, to seek out new life and new civilisations, to boldly go where no man has gone before'.

Even the self-discovery/self-help industry is a major one in all the nations of earth; people are willing to make great sacrifices to discover the 'truth' about themselves and the world. All this is undoubtedly true but discovery is much more than this and we will need to have a broader and more sophisticated understanding to undertake our studies of the texts set for study.

The Board of Studies has outlined in their documentation: students are required to 'explore the ways in which the concept of discovery is represented in and through texts'. (p9 *HSC Prescriptions 2015-20 English Stage 6*). This is our first step and it indicates that we must pay particular attention to the text and its content and techniques, particularly the techniques the composer uses to engage the audience and convey the main purpose of their text.

The whole aim of this Area of Study is to examine the text closely but also relate it to the idea of discovery and decide how examining it in this way enables us to better understand both the text and the concept. It is important that you formulate your own ideas about the text and attempt to develop some original and creative ideas about what you are studying.

The Board's documentation should be read in full and the annotations document should also be examined for the particular texts you are studying as this document offers insights into the way each particular text should be examined by outlining key ideas and areas for clarification.

The *Prescriptions* document states on the Area of Study that *Discovery* can be:

- something new
- a rediscovery
- sudden, unexpected
- carefully planned
- 'fresh and intensely meaningful in ways that may be emotional, creative, intellectual, physical and spiritual.' (p9)

- confronting
- provocative
- enable speculation

It can:

- change perceptions of individuals and groups.
- create new values

The document also suggests that discoveries and ways of discovering vary due to individual circumstance and that these discoveries can change many things about lives, communities and the world(s). Of course when we examine the concept of discovery we need to examine how 'discovering' the text itself may change us and how we view things. The text may challenge and confront and change how we see the human experience.

Students can also think about 'their own experiences of discovery' and how a composer's choice of form, feature and language influences their views of discovery. Examining and enjoying any text is a discovery in itself but it is what we take away from the text and apply that is the real discovery. That is not to say that every text will be enjoyed or offer a discovery. Some may not personally engage you and that is fine. This is especially so when you begin to find other related material that links to Discovery. Find examples of texts that link in significant ways to your prescribed text.

Defining Discovery

'Definition is the death of discovery'

-TOM SHADYAK

Now let's define discovery in a more coherent and easily understood way so we can begin our investigation at a basic level before moving into more complex analysis. Dictionary.com defines the term as:

1. The act or instance of discovering
2. Something discovered
3. In legal terms it is compulsory disclosure of evidence
4. The name of the third space shuttle.

Obviously the first three terms are more suitable but the final definition shows how pervasive the idea of discovery is and how it has influenced people over time. The search for the 'new' has driven much development over past millennia. Discoveries are always met with excitement and often trepidation as to what change they might bring.

Think historically about how people have reacted to change. It can cause great upheavals in society, with violent reactions while other changes brought through discoveries are welcomed and may save and enhance lives. Consider medical advancements, scientific developments and the ever-quickening world of the computer. Even the way I am creating this text in Evernote on an iPad would not have been possible twelve months ago. Discovery brings change and may affect different people or groups of people, even nations in various ways both positive and negative. It is pertinent now to examine some more definitions.

The word discover and its definition also sheds some light on the concept:

1. To see, get knowledge, to learn, to find, get knowledge of something previously seen or unknown.

As does the definition of the word discovering:

1. Noticing or realising.

These definitions all point to the fact that realisation is the key to discovery. This realisation may come unexpectedly, occasionally or never. Someone else may have the same experience and make the discovery. The realisation may be accidental or organised, take years in the planning or come as a complete surprise.

Discoveries can come in many ways and the synonyms for discover listed below help us to understand the concept even further. They assist in defining how a discovery can arise:

Synonyms – ascertain, catch, come upon, contrive, determine, design, dig up, disclose, elicit, explore, bring to light, unearth, encounter, experiment, invent, originate, expose, locate, perceive, sense, strike, verify.

These synonyms show partly the vast array of words that our language has created around this concept and show how important it is in the human psyche. Look also at the antonyms that show how we view not discovering things; lose, miss, pass by.

We, as a race, want to discover. Now we will look at some examples of discovery and examine their impact. It is also important to remember that discoveries do not have to be positive. You might discover you have a huge problem, an incurable illness, a strange past, an unwelcome relative or something equally bizarre. There may be a darker side to any discovery that could be addressed. Think about the effect of the white discoverers on indigenous populations.

Types of Discovery

Personal Discovery

'I think a spiritual journey is not so much a journey of discovery. It's a journey of recovery. It's a journey of uncovering your own inner nature. It's already there.'

BILLY CORGAN

The idea of personal discovery or self-discovery as many of the books also describe it, is a popular and pervasive concept. It is more prevalent in the developed nations of the world where people seek something more spiritual or meaningful rather than their consumer driven lives and the day to day grind of work. Many seek something more; they strive to discover something within or without, a better self, a way to live in the now or just a way to escape from reality. A huge amount of material (literature, DVDs, audiobooks) has been assembled to help individuals achieve their life goals.

Individuals seek to achieve personal discovery in a variety of ways. Some examples are courses and conferences where they are led through exercises, both physical and psychological, to develop new skills and discover their inner spirituality. Others join communities, religious groups or renounce material possessions and become itinerant travellers or, in old fashioned terms, 'hippies'. Through this they discover whatever they lack in their current state (hopefully) and become a better or more effective person. Others use these discoveries to enrich themselves or manage better in their existing lives. Whatever the reason or outcome, personal discovery is a huge industry and an integral part of our society.

For more information on this area you could investigate the self-help, self- improvement section of a book store or get on YouTube and type these terms in. You will get plenty of ideas and advice!

Inner Discovery

> *'The greatest discovery of my generation is that man can alter his life simply by altering his attitude of mind.'*
>
> **JAMES ADAMS**

The concept of inner discovery is closely aligned with the previous topic and can be seen similarly yet it is more aligned with exceptional circumstances. For example some people learn much about themselves during physical, emotional or psychologically stressful times and are astounded by the inner strength they have while others around them break down or fail to cope. Others find inner strength through meditation, retreats, or extremes such as becoming a hermit and focusing on the inner person. This concept of personal enlightenment is also a business in the modern world and you can get coaches who will work with you to find your inner self through various processes of discovery.

If you are looking for examples to use in your related material try googling the term and you will find a whole range of programs, coaches and books that will help you find your inner self. Dag Hammarskjold (former UN Secretary General) said 'The longest journey is the journey inwards. Of him who has chosen his destiny, who has started upon his quest for the source of his being.'

Discovery through Travel

The idea of discovery through travel is one of the first things that occur to people when they hear the word discovery. As Martin Buber (Austrian-born 20th Century Jewish philosopher) stated, 'All journeys have secret destinations of which the traveller is unaware'. This sense of travel enabling discoveries is well documented and became even more prominent as people began to sail widely across the seas to discover 'new' lands, many of which had been occupied by indigenous peoples for centuries. Travel was, and to some extent still is, associated with an adventure, a journey, to test the boundaries of what we already know and to see how far we can take the new experience and how it changes us. What we discover on our travels is revealing and often confronting.

> *Adventure is a path. Real adventure—self-determined, self-motivated, often risky—forces you to have firsthand encounters with the world. The world the way it is, not the way you imagine it. Your body will collide with the earth and you will bear witness. In this way you will be compelled to grapple with the limitless kindness and bottomless cruelty of humankind—and perhaps realise that you yourself are capable of both. This will change you. Nothing will ever again be black-and-white.*
>
> – **MARK JENKINS**
>
> (HTTP://MATADORNETWORK.COM/BNT/50-MOST-INSPIRING-TRAVEL-QUOTES-OF-ALL-TIME/#RCM3GIDFT04P07MB.99)

Discovery through travel brings this kind of change and it may involve understanding another culture, disrupting a prejudice or habit, making a friend or discovering some amazing natural beauty. Discovery through travel is one of the most written about and frequently mentioned ideas when discussing the concept. Travel has certainly changed over the centuries, even in the past decade travel to distant places has become commonplace. Air travel has especially become less than the special thing for the privileged or extremely adventurous that it was in the beginning. Think back to the times when to travel from place to place by foot or by horse was a major event. From the Middle Ages through to the later eighteenth century many people had never ventured beyond their village, apart from an infrequent trip to the nearest town. This idea leads us to consider the idea of the journey.

Discovery through Journey

This is an idea common to many areas of the discovery concept. Often the two words are associated if we think of the journey as a process not just a physical movement. Often discoveries are made on the journey rather than at the destination. The word journey has also been applied to abstract concepts. Lyndon Johnson, the American President, described peace as a deliberate process: 'Peace is a journey of a thousand miles and it must be taken one step at a time'. Many have heard the quote by Lao Tzu 'A journey of a thousand miles must begin with one step'.

The concept of journey leading to discovery is a constant in modern film and literature and it has been extensively studied in works such as Joseph Campbell's *The Hero's Journey*. This model organises the journey by stages which are common to all culture. Despite the cross-cultural commonalities, journeys allow discovery about self and such discoveries are individual.

As Marcel Proust (19th and 20th Century French novelist) stated, 'We don't receive wisdom; we must discover it for ourselves after a journey that no one can take for us or spare us.'

The physical journey could be local, in the same country, overseas or even in space, a place many science fiction texts take us. Fantasy writers create journeys of discovery in worlds of imagination and invention. Film also focuses on the concept of discovery through journey as we see in the range of road trip movies that seem so appealing to teen audiences. More serious films examine personal independence, the human condition and how one can discover something on the journey that will change or even save humanity. You will find many examples of this in film but try and choose something where the discovery has some significant personal and/or social impact and you can discuss techniques. Consider the idea of the journey as being inextricably linked to the concept of discovery as you make your way through the Area of Study.

Scientific and Technological Discovery

'Scientists have become the bearers of the torch of discovery in our quest for knowledge'

STEPHEN HAWKING

Regarding areas of discovery, foremost in many people's thoughts are the breakthroughs made in science and technology. They have immediate and significant impacts on modern day individuals and the way they interface with the world.

Examples of the impact of technology include:

- increased internet usage leading to the rise of social networking.
- miniaturisation of hand-held devices such as the iPad enabling people to communicate easily and more often.

- rapid changes in the way that data is stored such as the increased use of cloud-storage services has facilitated the development of much more flexible devices.

Einstein pointed out 'The process of scientific discovery is, in effect, a flight from wonder.' This is central to much of the debate that has raged over science in the past century or so. How do we progress scientifically and technologically and still maintain a moral and ethical basis? Should we chase many of the ideas that have arisen? For example the machines of war, the chemicals that kill and the genetic manipulations that can lead to social engineering are discoveries with ethical implications. Should there be limits and controls and if so how much? Discoveries can be fraught with danger on many levels.

While it is part of discovery to imagine and test the boundaries and seek new ways, it is also probably integral to human nature. With these new technologies the consequences are even greater than in the past as more people can be affected, more invasively and quickly. Dangers emerge as people discover new methods of being destructive, such as invading computers to distort programs with viruses or stealing through cybercrimes. These examples highlight that discoveries are not always positive.

Humanity must also grapple with the discovery of things such as climate change and environmental issues that are the result of industrialisation through discovered technologies. The consequences of many of the discoveries in the latter half of the last century are still being felt and new discoveries are needed to solve these problems. Discovery can be cyclical, inter-related and never-ending. Google '2014 Shift Happens' and watch a YouTube clip highlighting the rapid rate of discovery and change in this modern era!

Discovery as Creating New From Old

This is an intriguing idea probably best summed up in the idea of recycling materials to create something new. Old tyres can be used as soft fall for children's playgrounds, old ideas can be given new form, new ways can be thought up to approach a topic. Even just drawing attention to a common feature can enable people to discover something about it. This form of discovery is seen as creativity.

One example might be the light show Vivid which featured in Sydney. Prominent buildings such as the Opera House were illuminated with an exciting coloured light show. The buildings around the harbour foreshores were visible and bathed in psychedelic colours. People flocked to see the spectacle and the show received great reviews. The reactions evoked by the light show captured the idea of discovery and re-invention as otherwise familiar images were seen in an entirely new way. The sense of wonder and amazement experienced by young children observing the show was evidence of their discovery.

Sometimes a newly discovered thing can be as simple as reading a novel previously read or re-watching a film seen years before and getting something new or different from it. Great artists always borrow from the past and rearrange old elements into new discoveries for their audiences. Ideas such as this have led to new movements in the Arts or new methods of approaching a topic that casts new light on it. Postmodern texts such as the film *The Matrix*, use intertextuality as a key aspect.

Learning as Discovery

Learning in itself is a discovery that can make significant changes to an individual or a group. When we learn something that can be applied it is a small but potentially significant discovery for the individual or group. One significant piece of learning was the manipulation of fire, another the growing of crops, developing shelter and so on. While these are major discoveries other learning can be especially important for the individual. One example might be a breakthrough in reading or the ability to analyse and manipulate information to create something new. Consider this aspect of discovery as it can link to the other areas and be useful as an overriding idea to utilise as a thesis for the Area of Study essay.

Detection as Discovery

> *The basis of drama is... The struggle of the hero toward a specific goal at the end of which he realises that what kept him from it was, in the lesser drama, civilisation and, in the greater drama, the discovery of something that he did not set out to discover but which can be seen retrospectively as inevitable.*
>
> **DAVID MAMET**

The concept of detection as discovery is the integral aspect of the success of the eternally popular crime fiction genre and is also a major aspect of thrillers and similar literature, film and the visual arts. Paintings, for example, prove excellent material, to demonstrate how an individual can deduce something different from the same work as the person next to them. Detection, however, in its truest form is highly valued by audiences as it is about discovering the truth through clues.

Much literature has been written in this quest to make sense of a world where justice sometimes appears to be lacking. Of course the detective genre has changed much over the years and these variations have come to suit changing audiences and contexts but this search has rarely varied despite the form in which it is presented. Audiences love the sense of discovery in detection and an examination of any television or film guide will attest to the fact, as will an examination of library bookshelves.

"HOLMES GAVE ME A SKETCH OF THE EVENTS."

The Psychology of Discovery

'There'll always be serendipity involved in discovery'

JEFF BUZOS

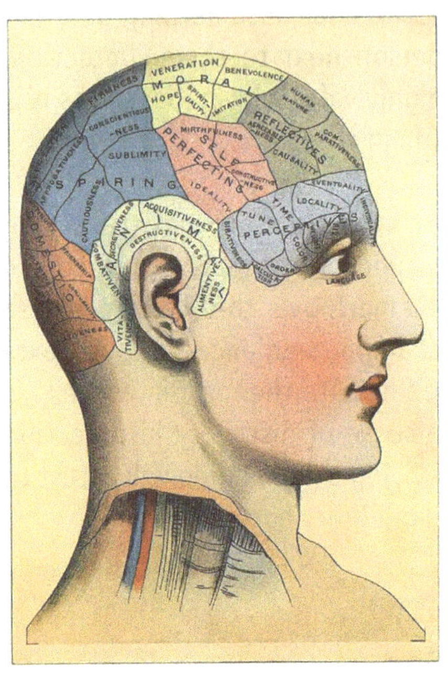

When I alluded to the innate need for discovery in the human psyche it wasn't superficial. The need for humanity to move ahead, to discover and to break boundaries is an important part of humanity's development and seems ingrained in us. The push to conquer new boundaries, to test, to push, to break boundaries is inherent in all development. Even if the discovery is the taste of a new food, the thrill of a new friend, or the discovery of any other sensory pleasure, it is a pleasure psychologically important to human development. The American writer Pearl S. Buck, who died in 1973, said that the basic discovery is the 'discovery of the relationship between men and women.' This is still true today. This quote could be used to explore the concept of discovery and to justify textual analysis from the perspective of feminist literary criticism. The field of Literary Criticism and new readings of texts is an example of boundary breaking.

There is something basic at an emotional level about discovery that attracts us to it. The new is important, broadening and thought provoking and this affects us on a psychological level. It is the emotional response that keeps people seeking the new, to discover and to absorb. This concept of the impact of discovery on our psyche is important as it is also a useful link to each of the texts and to your related material. It may be a useful concept to enable you to link your ideas together. Think about the basic psychological drives that motivate us and how they are important in all our discoveries.

Nationalism, Capitalism and other 'isms' as Drivers of Discovery

'People acting in their own self-interest is the fuel for all the discovery, innovation, and prosperity that powers the world'

JOHN STOSSEL

The idea that the 'isms' are drivers of discovery may not be appealing to some but there is no doubt that many of the discoveries of the last few centuries have been driven by them. One example is the race to land on the moon or the space race. This led to some awesome discoveries yet was driven by the great Cold War divide between the Communist Russian dictatorship and the American capitalist democratic system. Buoyed by the need to be first to set foot on the moon and discover what was there, billions were spent in making this happen.

Earlier still, the drive by nations such as Spain, Portugal and England to colonise the 'New World', particularly Africa and the Americas, led to many discoveries. National pride here was mixed with the drive for resources to support their ideology: religious, capitalist, communist or nationalist. This also led to many negatives such as exploitation in the race to conquer lands and spread 'civilisation'.

Capitalism, whatever your political belief, has been one of the greatest engines to drive discoveries over the centuries. This striving to produce product faster, more efficiently and thus, cheaply, has driven much innovation, prompted development of new technologies and resulted in new products. The instinct to improve and achieve is driven to its purest form by the capitalist system. It is not prudent here to discuss the pros and cons of the system itself but rather to recognise that it is a consummate motivator to Discovery. Gordon Gecko's quote from the film, *Wall Street*, sums up this philosophy brilliantly,

> *'Greed is right, greed works. Greed clarifies, cuts through and captures the essence of the evolutionary spirit. Greed in all of its forms; greed for life, for money, for love, knowledge has marked the upward surge of mankind.'*

Again relevant to this is the consideration of further analysing texts through the lens of literary criticism. For example, Marxist and New Historicist readings present different interpretations and may offer responders new insights and discoveries regarding texts.

Negative Aspects of Discovery

While it is common to have a positive image of discovery it is important to remember that it has negative aspects as well. For example, many of the early explorers who set out to discover new lands ended up dead. History is littered with such examples and many have gone down as glorious failures. One example is the story of Burke and Wills in Australia but you could also examine the exploration of the Antarctic and Arctic which have many failed expeditions. Other negatives can be found in the concept of discovering dreams of riches such as El Dorado or King Solomon's Mines.

The 'discovery' of new lands by European adventurers led to the exploitation of discovered natural resources. Indigenous peoples, considered uneducated savages, were often enslaved. The 'slave trade' was a negative by-product of this period of exploitation and discovery.

Away from this idea of exploration we can also have negatives in discoveries which yield promise such as nuclear power. This 'clean fuel' has been used for destructive purposes and Oppenheimer has said of his team's creation of the atomic bomb that it was a mistake. Many discoveries have been used negatively in war and in commerce for power and/or gain. We have even experienced psychological discoveries being used for brainwashing and other pernicious purposes. We have also mentioned the 'isms' that drive discovery and these can be negatively used as well. Communism killed millions and enslaved nations, patriotism in its extreme can lead to discovery but has impacted negatively on native populations and led to war.

Remember when you select a text for your related material or study a text there may be negatives to engage with that will enhance your understanding of the concept of discovery. Look for them to broaden your knowledge and ability to write clearly and formulate your own opinions.

Afterword on Discovery

'The pace of discovery is going unbelievably fast'

JAMES WATSON

Discovery is also about **possibility**, the idea that something in an imagination can be made real and attainable. Discovery is sometimes seeing the obvious and making use of it. Above all it entails faith/dreaming and an insatiable curiosity. When you read about many discoveries they are truly tales of failure with one success. Many stories tell of years of pain, toil, ridicule, dismal progress and rejection before success is achieved. Edison made a thousand bulbs before he got one to work. Failure is a constant with many people you will study in this topic until they discover their dream. They maintained their faith in the face of great adversity and this is what makes them discoverers. If it were easy everyone would do it!

Discoverers are also people who see what others have missed. Often they simply look at something in a new way. To look for new ideas, we must maintain an open mind. To discover for ourselves the mysteries of texts and how to unlock them, we must develop strategies for analysis and perseverance to achieve understanding.

Perhaps you think everything has been discovered as a pessimist might, but discoverers are optimists, people who continually seek success, or insight in achieving their goals or realising their dreams.

Questions for Discovery

- Define the term 'discovery' in your own words.
- How can discovery and possibility be connected?
- Discuss what the term discovery means to you.
- Create your own list of synonyms and antonyms for the word discovery. Then, choose two or three to use in your writing so the word discovery won't be repeated.
- Science is often connected with discovery. Research one such instance and write two paragraphs on it connecting it thematically to your set text.
- What is positive about discovery?
- Discuss the idea that discovery can be a two-edged sword.
- Discuss one discovery and the benefits of that discovery to humanity.
- Do you think the concept of discovery is integral to detective fiction? Explain your answer fully.
- Analyse one 'ism' and how discovery has been driven by it.
- Discuss some of the negatives associated with the concept of discovery.

STUDYING A NON-FICTION TEXT

The medium of a text is very important. If a text is non-fiction this means that its purpose is to report or represent events, people, situations or trends. Realism is achieved in a non-fiction text through reference to actual people, events or situations. These may be reported or discussed objectively or subjectively. A non-fiction text is not created in the same way as a novel; the composer does not imagine the characters and events and dialogue is not invented. Rather, the composer of a non-fiction text shapes the text by choosing which events to include and how he or she portrays them. The manner of this portrayal will depend on the composer's purpose. The composer adds his or her perspective to the description of the events and this perspective or even bias will have an effect on the way the responder perceives the material. The responder can choose to accept or reject the composer's version of events.

The creator of a non-fiction text, like the composer of a fiction text, will create interest through the use of language techniques. These are the elements of the text which are manipulated by the composer in order to present ideas effectively. When you are discussing how the composer of a written text represents ideas, you must discuss language techniques. Language techniques are sometimes referred to as stylistic devices. Many language techniques used in non-fiction are identical to those used in fiction. See more on this topic in the section titled 'Language'.

THE CONTEXT

It is very important for you to have an understanding of the context. This includes an understanding of both the time and place linked to the text's content and the time and place from which the text originated. Such knowledge can assist readers to appreciate fully the elements of discovery in this text. There are layers of discovery, both physical and inner, and these are made by multiple characters. However, without an understanding of the historical, social and political context, as well as the personal context of the composer, you will not be able to bring a sophisticated understanding to your responses.

Many of Guevara's reflections centre on the plight of the indigenous and working class people of Latin America. Therefore, an understanding of the history of the people is extremely important. The journey starts in Argentina, one of the most southern countries in South America with a culture quite distinctive from other parts of South and Central America.

Prior to Colonisation

Before colonisation, Central and South America was inhabited by indigenous South Americans whose cultures were ancient and highly revered. Society was agricultural based, with people living off what they could grow and trade with other towns. However, they were in no way 'backward' or uncivilised. In fact, while London was fighting the plague and other diseases as a result of poor sewage and town planning, some tribes of Central and South America lived in impressive towns with full sewage, garbage collection and a highly organised system of government based mostly on a military hierarchy. You may have learnt about some of these groups, such as the Aztecs, the Mayans and the Incas in Junior History.

These three civilisations were extremely advanced. These people understood the importance of infrastructure, particularly as they embarked on empire building. This required them to develop complicated systems of taxation and administration which can all be seen in their meticulous record keeping in codex. While they did not write as such, they used pictures to indicate monetary value and to express their administrative systems and their beliefs about their gods. These peoples were exceptional artisans, producing beautifully coloured woven rugs and pottery and they became advanced hunters and gatherers. These tribes all shared a similar culture but cannot be classified as the same people. In fact, they were often at war with each other as they sought to expand their empires. In Argentina, there were various tribes as the country was never entirely occupied by one dominant tribe like Mexico for example, which was ruled by the Aztecs.

Colonisation and Warfare

The Spanish attempted to colonise Argentina in the 1500s, as they did much of Central and South America. However, the indigenous people resisted the take-over and successfully retained the southernmost area of Argentina. This helped to sustain their culture. Yet, the country was given its current Spanish name, Argentina, and the capital was called Buenos Aires. The official language became Spanish, making this country one of the largest Spanish speaking nations. Some tribes, particularly in the mountains, continued to live in their traditional ways. The Argentinians fiercely resisted colonial take-over by the British in the 1800s and began to weaken their ties with the Spanish as the Spanish Empire declined. However, the traditional ways of the native Argentinians were being lost as governments changed and they were forced to modernise with their traditional culture being impacted by new railways and trade.

Argentina was one of the top ten wealthiest nations at the beginning of the 1900s. However, when the Wall Street Crash occurred in the 1920s, Argentina suffered, along with the rest of the Americas. This was the Argentina that Ernesto Guevara was born into in 1928. (See more in 'The Composer' section).

During the 1930s, the army often fought the government. This was known as a revolution or a coup. While, technically, elections were held, there was a lot of corruption in the government, with some parties being banned from participating in the election and officers being appointed without a formal election. This sort of corruption often meant that the people of Argentina were essentially powerless in terms of electing who they wanted in their government positions. They were unable to improve their situation of poverty and unemployment as they were denied a say in government.

Peronism

One of the turning points in Argentina's history was a military coup held in 1943 which eventually led to the election of a man called Juan Peron in 1946. Guevara talks about Peron and Peronism in *The Motorcycle Diaries* so it is worth knowing a little bit about Peron and what he did for Argentina that so inspired Guevara.

Peron was formerly the Minister for Welfare, however, because he was so popular with the workers, he posed a threat to the government and he was consequently jailed. The people of Argentina protested openly for his freedom and he was eventually released. It was no surprise then, given his popularity amongst the workers and the common people, that he was elected President in 1946.

Peron and his wife, Eva Peron, were exceptionally popular amongst the people of Argentina as the government introduced many welfare policies to help the poorer people in the country. Under Peronism, conditions and wages for workers improved and unemployment was almost non-existent. However, all of these policies cost a lot of money and resulted in the economic decline of the country. Eva Peron fought for women's suffrage (the vote for women) and for the most vulnerable people in society. Her early death from cancer in 1952 threw Argentina into deep mourning. Peron was re-elected as President. However, as a result of assassination attempts and a coup designed to oust him from power, he decided to resign and he then lived in exile in Spain.

The new government formed after the coup banned anything associated with Peron and Peronism. However, many of the people, particularly the lower classes and workers, continued to fight for Peron's dream of a fairer society. These 'underground' groups met in secret and were often referred to as revolutionaries as they intended to take back the government of Argentina for the people.

PANAMA CANAL
CARACAS
VENEZUELA
BOGOTA
COLOMBIA
GUIANA
ECUADOR
Cuenca
Amazon R.
Trujillo
PERU
LIMA
BOLIVIA
Lake Titicaca
LA PAZ
Potosí
BRAZIL
PACIFIC OCEAN
CHILE
PARAGUAY
ASUNCION
RIO DE JANEIRO
São Paulo
ARGENTINA
Valparaiso
URUGUAY
MONTEVIDEO
BUENOS AIRES
ATLANTIC OCEAN

THE COMPOSER

Early Background

Ernesto Rafael Guevara de la Serna was born in Rosario Argentina, on June 14th 1928. He was born at a time when the economy was suffering and political tensions were high, as they would be for many years to come. His parents have been described as 'left leaning' meaning that, in terms of politics, they supported the more radical movement of government, rather than the conservative side. Another way of putting this is that they disliked the corruption they saw in the government and felt that more should be done for the people of Argentina who lived in poverty with very little power. They were very open at home about their political ideas and were highly supportive of their son's clear 'left leanings' as well. Ernesto Guevara became interested in politics at a young age and would participate in protests. His father openly supported militant revolutionaries by protecting them and allowing them to hide out in their home.

Guevara had asthma as a child which, in those days, could significantly impact someone's life as they did not have the same medication and health advice that we have in the Western world today. However, he was very athletic and highly successful in sports, such as rugby. He would go on to become quite a successful soldier, despite his asthma.

Political Influences

Karl Marx

The young Ernesto Guevara was an avid reader and the family home held an extensive library of about 3,000 books. His favourite authors shed some insight into the man he would become. He loved Jack London who greatly admired the natural landscape in America and inspired the romanticist ideals held by Ernesto. These values included a deep appreciation for nature, freedom and beauty.

Ernesto also read political books by authors such as Engels and Marx, who are now known as the fathers of communism. Communism is a form of government where all wealth is shared equally so there is no class system, that is, no poor class and no wealthy class. Everything is shared and everyone is equal, whether you are a doctor or a factory worker. This ideology appealed to Ernesto as he believed that wealth and power should be distributed more equally in Argentina, rather than the poor being left without appropriate government support and being voiceless in terms of changing their government.

The only option he saw for the people to change their government was through military or violent means as the election system had become corrupt. Guevara was highly intellectual to the point that even the American CIA noted this in his case file and saw his intellect as a threat.

Journeys of Discovery

In 1948, Guevara, aged 20, decided to study medicine and he enrolled at the University of Buenos Aires. He would often take time from his studies, however, to travel and explore Latin America. Guevara took several journeys in his life which fundamentally changed who he was. These journeys were seen as catalysts for self-discovery. The first was his solo journey through the north provinces of Argentina which he commenced in 1950 and where he covered approximately 4,500kms. His second trip in 1951 is the trip upon which he takes us in *The Motorcycle Diaries*. In this trip, he took a year off from his studies and toured with his friend, Alberto Granado, for nine months around South America. It was on this second journey he discovered the full extent of the suffering of the people of Latin America. He would later take a third journey, his second around Latin America with Granado, but this journey is not covered in this text.

Political and Military Life after *The Motorcycle Diaries*

As a result of the journey that Guevara outlines in *The Motorcycle Diaries*, as well as other contextual influences, Guevara would go on to become one of the most famous revolutionaries in South America. His medical background, along with his exceptional strategic mind for military campaigns, allowed him to be extremely useful to groups of revolutionaries wishing to overthrow corrupt governments. During 1954, influenced by his journey outlined in *The Motorcycle Diaries*, Guevara went to Guatemala where he witnessed a government trying to implement socialist reforms. Uncultivated portions of large landholdings were expropriated and given to landless peasants so they could earn a living or, at best, grow food to feed their families. During this time, Guevara focussed on making connections with other like-minded people and learning how to enact real change in a country.

Through his connections in Guatemala, Guevara met Fidel Castro, a famous revolutionary in history who deposed the American-backed Batista regime to install a communist government in Cuba in 1955. Guevara played an integral role in this Cuban revolution. His experiences in 1951 and 1952 (described in *The Motorcycle Diaries)* and his observations in Guatemala were no doubt influential in his self-discovery and development as a political activist and revolutionary doctor. (He graduated from medical school in 1953). At this time, Guevara was given the nickname 'Che' which is a form of speech used by the Argentinians in everyday speech. While it formally translates as 'friend', it can be likened to the way New Zealander's use the word 'bro', and Australians use the word 'mate'. Che, as he was now known, became a central figure in the formation of the new Communist government of Cuba.

International Influence

Guevara travelled around the world, speaking of his experiences and his beliefs. He spoke at the United Nations General Assembly (December 11, 1964) of his passion for social equality. His message was addressed particularly to nations, such as the United States of America, whom he saw as having a government which took advantage of people living in third world conditions. He also travelled to the Congo in Africa where he actively supported a revolutionary coup.

Guevara intended to continue to support other revolutionaries who wanted to overthrow their governments. However, due to his rising profile and his desire to liberate much of Latin America from corrupt governments, he was considered a person of threat to the major capitalist governments at the time, particularly, the United States of America.

Guevara's Death and Legacy

By 1966, Guevara had to travel under disguises as the United States Government saw him as a political enemy and wanted to remove his influence. During a military expedition in Bolivia in 1967, Guevara was wounded and captured, along with other guerrilla fighters. The Bolivian special forces who were trained and supported by the CIA, executed Guevara at the direction of the Bolivian president and his remains were buried in an unknown location. He was 39 years old.

In 1997, Ernesto 'Che' Guevara's remains were located and returned to Cuba where they remain. An elaborate memorial was erected to him there and he still holds iconic status throughout Latin America, and the world, today. He has become a symbol of resistance but also an iconic symbol of freedom at any cost. His face is printed on t-shirts wearing his signature beret with a red star representing his communist and revolutionary values.

DIARY ENTRIES – SUMMARIES AND ANALYSIS

Prefaces

The Motorcycle Diaries contains a helpful introduction prior to the actual text by Guevara. The preface, written by his daughter, Aleida Guevara March, sheds valuable insight into her experience of reading her father's account of such a significant time in his life. (It is worth noting that Guevara's second wife was also called Aleida).

Guevara's daughter refers to her own discovery of her father as she read his diaries for the first time. She states that, as she read, she "began to see more clearly who this person was." She even imagines herself in the character of Granado, trying to gain a deeper understanding of her father.

She sees his journey as one of discovery and comments that he left to embark on his journey with particular goals and aspirations but these fundamentally changed along the way. She says that, "as he discovered the reality of our continent, [he] continued to mature as a human being and to develop as a social being." Along with this physical and associated social discovery of South America came self-discovery. His daughter reflected, "Slowly we see his dreams and ambitions change. He grew increasingly aware of the pain of many others and he allowed it to become part of himself."

She talks about how, as a result of this journey, one of the key things that her father discovered was his purpose in life in regards to his vocation. Prior to the journey, he was studying to become a doctor and was committed to this goal. In fact, one of the main aims of the journey was to gain experience with leprosy patients throughout Latin America. She pinpoints the change that occurred in Guevara as a result of his journey, “In his consciousness, the awareness grows that what poor people need is not so much his scientific knowledge as a physician, but rather his strength and persistence in trying to bring about social change that would enable them to live with the dignity that was taken from them and trampled on for centuries”. She believes that this journey not only changed his career path but fundamentally changed who he was. Guevara “shows us how reality, if properly interpreted, can permeate a human being to the point of changing his or her way of thinking.” His daughter’s comments and reflections link well to Discovery and such quotations are worth memorising as you study the text.

Not only does Aleida Guevara March identify Guevara’s self-discovery, as well as her own discovery of her father, she also acknowledges the discovery the audience can make about Guevara and the world. She claims that Guevara shows us, the audience, “a Latin America that few of us know about” suggesting that the audience too can achieve self-discovery in the form of knowledge, through the discovery of Guevara and his journey. Like Guevara’s own influences from books, the audience too can be fundamentally changed and discover more about themselves through witnessing Guevara’s own transformation within the pages of this text. When we discover places and values through reading about them rather than experiencing them first hand, this is called ‘vicarious experience.’

Aleida Guevara March’s preface ends on a note of sadness though as she challenges the audience that there is more to discover. She says that, if we were to retrace Guevara’s journey in modern times we would discover that not much had actually changed at all and, despite Guevara's sacrifice, there is still work to be done. She leaves us with the thought,"There is a challenge for those of us who – like this man who would years later become Che – are sensitive to the reality that so mistreats the most wretched among us, those of us who have a commitment to helping create a world that is much more just." In this way, the legacy of Che Guevara may continue and others may discover their purpose in life. They may also be to help those who are suffering.

Diaries are usually kept private. Why were these diary entries published? Is it so readers can experience self-discovery vicariously, through reading of Guevara's own personal transformation as a result of travel?

In the 'preface to the first edition' Aleida informs the audience about the process through which this text was constructed. This process of construction and structure is an important element of your understanding of the text. She reveals that Guevara kept a travel diary throughout his journey with Granado. Guevara himself re-wrote the diaries in a narrative form, allowing for reflection on the impact that the events had on him at the time and, as Aleida states, "offering the reader a deeper insight into Che's life, especially at a little known stage, and revealing details of his personality, his cultural background and his narrative skill." Thus the diary entries recount, reflect and, relevant to the issue of discovery, reveal.

The reader is able to discover the thoughts of the writer and we "witness the extraordinary change which takes place in him as he discovers Latin America, gets right to its very heart and develops a growing sense of Latin American identity." Thus, while the book is called *The Motorcycle Diaries*, it is also part memoir. Good memoirs reflect on experiences and represent identity.

Other useful elements prior to the central text

It is a good idea to make sure you understand what Guevara went on to do after this journey as the discoveries that he makes on this journey significantly influenced the rest of his life. In order to have a deep understanding of the concept of discovery in this text, you need to know how his discoveries impacted his life. While this can be found in the chronological snapshots of his life and the brief biography provided, more research and reading into this area is advised (see 'Context' and 'The Composer' sections of this guide).

It is advisable to print out a map of Latin America as this allows you to visualise the journey of Guevara and helps you to understand key plot points throughout the text. The itinerary of *The Motorcycle Diaries* provides a clear image of how far they travelled through all the different towns and countries and how long they were away for on their journey. Note – there is a small map included prior to the itinerary section in the 2014 Ocean Press edition.

The introduction by Cintio Vitier, a renowned Cuban literary figure, offers even more insight into the text and the transformative themes within it. This section provides several valuable quotes about the text and the theme of discovery as Vitier sees this journey as Guevara's "awakening" as "we can see the origins of the budding revolutionary in Che." Guevara's journey and the idea of awakening is closely linked to Discovery and rubric terms such as, 'confronting', 'provocative', 'intensely meaningful.'

The journey involved, 'changed perceptions of things,' not least Guevara's own changed view of himself and his place in the world. This text may also help you discover this historical figure and may change your own social and political views as you are challenged and confronted and discover new ways to perceive the human experience.

The Motorcycle Diaries: Notes on a Latin American Journey

Some notes on structural elements of the text

The text's subtitle emphasises that the central focus of the text is a journey through Latin America. This is the catalyst for all of the discoveries that follow. This is a text where the discoveries about others, the country and self, all come from the physical journey that was undertaken. This may align or contrast with your other texts but should be something that you consider when comparing texts and selecting related material. Not all of your texts will have the same catalyst for discovery, particularly self-discovery so this can be a valuable discussion point in your integrated response.

Each diary entry begins with a Spanish heading and then its English translation. These headings serve to remind the reader that *The Motorcycle Diaries* was written in Spanish. The headings can give us, the audience, insight as to what Guevara saw as the central or most significant element of each entry. You are reminded to use the term, 'diary entries' rather than chapters in your own writing on the text.

We are also provided with some photographs in the middle of the text as evidence for Guevara's journey and the people he meets along the way. This section serves to lend authenticity to the text and allows us to visualise the journey more clearly, thus increasing the connection between Guevara and his readers. These photos increase the engagement for responders as they can visualise his journey and see his transformation from wearing dress pants and a tie, to his more casual attire when in the leper colonies and on the raft sailing down the Amazon River. Thus, the discoveries Guevara makes are reflected visually through his changed attire. Finally, the last photo reveals his transformed identity as he is wearing the iconic beret with the star, smoking a Cuban cigar and representing the people of Latin America in the international media. These photographs show, not just the physical evidence of the journey, but the transformation of Guevara himself as a result of the journey he undertook. They are a part of the published text and you are advised not to ignore them. They can be analysed using visual literacy techniques. As mentioned, these contrasting high modality images may well reflect aspects of discovery for the subject. For example, compare the fourth image with the last, along with the caption and discuss aspects of Discovery raised. The visuals have been carefully selected to complement the written text.

In terms of physical composition, the text is structured as a series of sequential diary entries, a narrative technique that Guevara has chosen. The entries are not numbered. He could have kept the text as the original diary, but the final text was edited by Guevara with the benefit of hindsight and reflection at the conclusion of the journey. This is a significant technique; the inclusion of an older, reflective narrative voice which, coming from the advantage of hindsight, helps to highlight the self-discoveries made on the journey.

The text therefore, is not pure diary form as diaries are usually written shortly after the event and are often seen as a personal, daily record. This text includes autobiographical elements such as self-reflection and commentary. This blend of life-writing sub-genres may justify the use of the term 'hybrid genre' and this blending is seen in postmodern texts in particular. This can be a discussion point, particularly if you're asked a question that focusses on structure and techniques. There are aspects of narrative and several autobiographical elements within the text that you could discuss when you are talking about the techniques of composition. It is important to consider the additional components such as the preface, appendix and selection of photographs. Consider when and why the text was published and the impact of time on the telling.

Structural aspects are also important to consider when looking for related texts. Will you look for texts which are representative of a genre? Are there other published diaries which may also raise issues of self-discovery through journey, event or present challenges and discoveries for responders about a certain person, place and time in history?

The following section briefly summarises each diary entry.

so we understand each other

"This is not a story of heroic feats, or merely the narrative of a cynic; at least I do not mean it to be. It is a glimpse of two lives running parallel for a time, with similar hopes and convergent dreams."

In this introduction to his journey of discovery, Guevara advises the reader that the notes are his personal account of this nine month adventure, which he has reorganised with the benefit of hindsight.

He acknowledges that the text represents only his own perspective. He uses a metaphor to articulate his point that “it is likely that out of 10 possible heads I have seen only one true tail.” He goes on to say that he can describe what his eyes have seen but that it is impossible for his audience to truly see through his own eyes. “Readers of this book will not be well versed in the sensitivity of my retina.” Guevara states it will be up to the audience to trust him, “You can either believe me, or not”.

Guevara’s acknowledgement of his limitations in terms of form and singular perspective allows the relationship between the composer and the reader to be very honest and open from the beginning. The singular perspective offered through a travel diary written by one person, albeit a younger and older voice of that person incorporating reflection from hindsight, relates closely to Discovery. Guevara does not pretend to be an omniscient narrator, nor does he plan to try and convince his audience that his truth is the only truth. Instead he invites the reader to share his experiences and discoveries and then, if they don’t believe him, to go on the journey themselves and see if they can find an alternative truth. As this is a non-fiction text, the audience can have a more personal relationship with Guevara where he can use direct address to establish a relationship of trust and authenticity. This is a technique that will no doubt provide you with a distinction between this prescribed text and your related material if your related material is fictional.

Guevara lets us know that he has been profoundly changed by this journey: "The person who wrote these notes passed away the moment his feet touched Argentine soil again...I'm not the person I once was." This is a stellar quote to reveal that the journey changed Guevara. He says so and his words reveal that the journey involved self-discovery. This is not a presumption or interpretation on the part of the reader, it is an admission by the author. We are told directly. The physical journey exposed deep social injustices. These, in turn, were a catalyst for an inner discovery and complete transformation for the composer.

By acknowledging the transformation from the outset, the reader becomes aware that Guevara will be likely to use reflection and hindsight as he recounts his journey. Thus a reflective style of writing is significant in conveying the concept of discovery.

As responders, we are allowed to witness the discoveries that were made and, most importantly, Guevara's reflections regarding how those discoveries changed him from his self-declared, "man I used to be" to the person he became.

forewarnings

In this second diary entry, Guevara outlines how the journey began. It is important to note the reasons why he wanted to explore and discover Latin America. We also gain an understanding of what he was like before his life-changing journey of discovery.

This diary entry records the way in which plans for the trip spontaneously evolved over a drink of 'mate' (the Argentinian national drink) shared by Guevara and Granado. The drinking of mate is a ritual to be repeated many times throughout *The Motorcycle Diaries*.

Both men were feeling disillusioned with life, were unemployed and keen to seek adventure. This was the original reason for their decision to head towards North America on Granado's motorbike, 'La Poderosa II' (literally 'The Mighty One'). Guevara notes that he was "feeling uneasy, more than anything because having the spirit of a dreamer I was particularly jaded with medical school, hospitals and exams."

This self-description is an apt quote to explain what he was like prior to his self-discovery. He describes how he was quite naïve before the journey which was largely based on, "improvisation." His youthful innocence is captured in the quote, "The enormity of our endeavour escaped us in those moments." This is a relevant quote also as one of the discoveries that Guevara makes along the way is how ill prepared they were for the journey they were undertaking and how challenging the landscape of his beloved South America could be. This sense of freedom and desire to travel is often described as wanderlust.

Another word you might read in relation to this text is 'Bildungsroman'. This is also known as a 'coming of age' story where one or more of the characters change throughout the text, moving from a state of naivety or innocence to one of more maturity and responsibility as a result of their experiences. The label is often reserved for fiction but there are definite overlaps with regard to the change that the protagonist experiences in this prescribed text.

The title given to this diary entry, could be a reference to the forewarnings they missed early on in their journey. (Remember Guevara has 'reorganised' and 'polished' his diary entries after the conclusion of the journey, the titles to each entries would be a later addition.) There is a foreshadowing in,

> *The enormity of our endeavour escaped us in those moments; all we could see was the dust on the road ahead and ourselves on the bike, devouring kilometres in our flight northward.*

This description encapsulates their looming discoveries and experience. Guevara, at this point, is unaware of the self-discoveries he will make and how they will change his identity.

discovery of the ocean

In the opening paragraph of this diary entry, Guevara vividly records Granado's first experience of the ocean. Herein lies an element of discovery. Note the language techniques he uses to describe the ocean.

The pair have contrasting responses to the ocean – for Guevara the ocean has always been metaphorically like "a confidant, a friend absorbing all it is told and never revealing those secrets." However, for his friend Granado, it is a new experience, a "strangely perturbing sight" and he is "overwhelmed" by the fact that this ocean "signifies an infinite number of paths to all ends of the earth." This emphasises the personal nature of discovery.

In this entry, we meet the little dog, Comeback who is Guevara's link to his girlfriend, Chichina. His relationship with her at the beginning of the text is very important. Indeed, he states, "a symbol of the union demanding my return". However, later in the journey, this relationship lessens in significance as Guevara's transformation occurs through his physical journey and his journey of self-discovery.

Guevara and Granado's growing awareness of the challenges they face on this journey can be seen in this diary entry. It is seen in the doubt expressed by people around them as well as in their own experience and apprehension. Guevara's uncle plans to buy a lottery ticket *if* they get to Bariloche, while others taunt them "that the bike would be a good excuse to go jogging".

According to Granado's plans, he thought the trip would be finished when they had only just begun. Their beloved Norton motorcycle proved to be very challenging to steer and they had many spills.

...lovesick pause

In this diary entry Guevara describes the difficulty he felt about leaving his girlfriend– this is a point of uncertainty and 'limbo' for him. Guevara uses intertextuality by including the poem by Otera Silva which reflects his own feelings about the difficulty of saying goodbye to the woman he loves. This example helps to highlight how his values later change so profoundly as a result of his discoveries. He did not appreciate how important this trip would be for him. At this stage, he still sees it as a simple adventure.

Guevara describes how he sat with his girlfriend by the ocean and this previously described "confidant" seemed to be warning him that it was time to leave. He states, "I heard the ocean's warning." It grows very cold, forcing a move from the beach back towards the commencement of his journey. He says that, "in the enormous belly of a Buick the bourgeois side of my universe was still under construction." It is his hindsight that leads him to reflect in this way because he is writing this memoir at the point after the journey when his discoveries have aligned him more with the working class struggle than with his more bourgeois origins. This is an example of how Guevara's discoveries impact the way he writes about himself and the journey once it has been completed. Thus, again, the narrative voice is a significant factor in foregrounding the concept of discovery in the text.

Another example of a change in thinking as a result of discovery is the bracelet. Granado encourages Guevara to ask for Chichina's bracelet, seemingly as a token of his connection with her. Guevara later discovers the need to see the bracelet as having monetary rather than sentimental value. This is again likened to bourgeois thinking where sentimental attachment to material things leads to people consuming more.

until the last tie is broken

Guevara's journey thus far is marked by hospitality from friends and family. In the previous diary entry, Guevara's uncle loaded them up with vegetables and threw meat to his dog. In this entry, they enjoy a steak lunch and "three days of the good life".

It is a good idea to learn some quotes attesting to the affluent lifestyle and relative comfort experienced by the young men at this point in the journey. This will enable you to make comparisons with their changed living conditions later in the text. Such juxtaposition will serve to contextualise and form a background to the discoveries they make.

Later in *The Motorcycle Diaries*, the young travellers discover what it is like to be hungry and to truly live like working class people. In this entry, Guevara notes that, "These were the last days in which we did not have to think about money." This is a turning point in his journey as it was not until they faced significant challenges on their journey that they were able to make discoveries about themselves and their world. Do your related texts also present the opportunity for discoveries to be made as a result of challenges?

We first hear about politics in this diary entry when the men stop to visit a friend of Granado's who is a member of the Radicals (the party representing the new urban and industrial classes, and also attracting some poorer people). Guevara does not see the Radicals as offering a "tenable political position."

They then begin to face more significant difficulties with the bike and navigating the terrain and experience numerous crashes. If you were to have a question focusing on challenges and Discovery within this text, think about which examples you could already use to support your points.

Despite physical challenges, the travellers remain optimistic. A quote from Guevara encapsulates his values and focus at this time. He states that, "Distant countries, heroic deeds and beautiful women spun around and around in our turbulent imaginations."

This is a useful quote as it can be compared with Guevara's values and focus at the end of the text to emphasise how his discoveries have profoundly changed him. At this point, it is clear that the motive for this journey is adventure and selfish experience. Hedonism and a desire to experience adventure may be said to have inspired the journey but the same values are not evident at the conclusion of the journey. The men know they are going to see a leper colony but Guevara describes this as 'heroic deeds' rather than humble service. He will discover that the places where he thinks he will be a hero are actually the places where he will discover the most about this continent that he knows little about, and about himself. This raises the issue that self-discovery can involve changed perspectives. He describes the world he left behind him, "mocking the so-called liberation I sought." He recognises, as a narrator with hindsight, that what he thought was the liberation he sought in terms of freedom of self and few responsibilities, was not the kind of liberation that he would encounter. His true liberation as a result of his discoveries would be the liberation of his own thinking from a focus on perceived self-gratification and pleasure to a devotion to alleviating the suffering of others, physically, emotionally and socially.

for the flu, bed

Once again, this diary entry opens with powerful imagery, "The bike exhaled with boredom along the accident free road and we exhaled with fatigue." The personification of the bike heightens the engagement for the reader and emphasises the challenges of the journey.

Guevara gets sick but once again they are treated "royally" by the local doctor who is able to get them back on the road within a few days. However, Guevara does note how their circumstances were soon to change significantly. He reflects on a photo that Alberto took of him and describes it as, "an acknowledgement of our changed circumstances and of the horizons we were seeking, free at last from 'civilisation'". This is another apt quote as it emphasises Guevara's initial reflections on the trip and highlights how naïve the young men were at the outset. He states that they took joy in the idea of freedom from civilisation. This was actually, however, a moment of naivety as they would go on to truly discover the practical implications of such freedom.

The rest of the entry describes the ongoing physical and mental challenges that they would suffer; the bike struggling, having to sleep on the side of the road, the inability to erect their tents in adverse weather conditions, minimal sleep, thirst and hunger. They do find some solace, however, when some German ranch owners allow them to take shelter with their workers in the farm labourer's kitchen. Here Guevara has his first contact with some of the working class people of the country. These workers belong to one of the native tribes of Chile known as the Araucanian people. Like many indigenous Latin Americans, they had their lands colonised by Spanish and European peoples and became a poorer class in their swiftly modernising country. Guevara notes their "deep suspicion of the white man who in the past has brought them so much misfortune and now continues to exploit them."

This is one of the first of many encounters with indigenous people recorded in *The Motorcycle Diaries*. It contributes to Guevara's self-discovery as he experiences first-hand the plight of his fellow man.

san martin de los andes

Guevara's sharply contrasting descriptions of natural beauty and the "unattractive, miserable town" reveal his appreciation of nature and provide a cynical view of physical discovery. He writes with an ironic tone, "the day it was 'discovered' as a tourist haven the town's climate and transport difficulties were solved and its subsistence secured."

Improvisations continue to work and the travellers are successful in securing accommodation and food. They savour the experience of San Martin and acknowledge that "travelling is our destiny."

Guevara also recognises that travelling is contributing to his growing understanding and as he looks to the future, he imagines later returning to Argentina, "if not indefinitely then at least for a pause while I shift from one understanding of the world to another." This quotation serves to highlight the theme of discovery through new learning, knowledge and changed understanding. This learning is based on a new social awareness.

The next anecdote reminds us that the two travellers are still young, innocent and without responsibility as they attend a barbeque and attempt to steal some wine for later consumption. Guevara discovers that he feels ashamed of the way he behaved as they had been treated with wonderful hospitality; however, they had not treated their hosts with the same respect. They admit to leaving with "our tails between our legs." They are both learning that they are actually still quite naïve in some respects.

circular exploration

This entry records another moment of discovery – of warm hospitality, friendships and the joy of nature.

Granado and Guevara visit a mining town and enjoy the hospitality of Granado's friends who treat them to an Argentinian feast as they get ready to farewell their country.

This entry also records in detail the moments of indulgence where the boys are able to enthusiastically explore their surroundings, hunt and simply enjoy nature.

Guevara reflects on the effect that the beauty of nature had on them in the words, "The tremor of nature cut straight to our hearts. We walked slowly so as not to disturb the peace of the wild sanctuary with which we were now communing." This description emphasises a moment of clarity and humility Guevara felt in the face of nature. Coupled with their experience in the previous diary entry, the young men are beginning to develop a more healthy respect for their environment, both physical and social.

dear mama

This entry is a letter Guevara wrote to his mother at this stage of the journey. Without going into details, he tells her of his brief illness and his experience with penicillin (a relatively new drug at that time). He also highlights the beauty of San Martin de los Andes. He deflects the challenges by saying that they used their "usual resourcefulness to solve the thousand problems that plagued us along the way". He shows that he is still thinking of his old life as he includes a page for his mother to give to his girlfriend, Chichina.

He is clearly excited about the medical discovery he has been able to make for a patient and details the tumour he identified.

These entries are providing examples of a different sensitivity, a response to those people and things around him.

on the seven lakes road

This entry again highlights Guevara's newly found appreciation for nature. This is seen through sensory descriptions such as, "the scent of wilderness caressing our nostrils." Guevara also shares his discovery that a deeper appreciation of the spirit of a place is possible if you stay for a few days. Hence the realisation is conveyed that it not so much the distance that is travelled, but it is the depth of experience that is important.

The young friends share mate with a "stoical pair" who have been camping by the edge of the lake for several days and who put their own efforts to shame.

In a moment of dark humour, Guevara and Granado have been made to feel scared about a wild puma in the area that was allegedly attacking people. The boys manage to get accommodation in a stable but are exceptionally fearful that they may be attacked by this wild animal. In an unfortunate turn of events, Guevara ends up shooting what he believes is a puma but what turns out to be the beloved dog of the owners of the property. Alberto had to get the bike fixed, leaving Guevara alone. He reflects, "I thought I'd have to spend the night in the open, being unable to ask for a bed in a house where we were considered murderers."

This anecdote gives the audience an insight into Guevara's sense of humour and also a sense of discovery of how fear and pressure cause him to act. He acknowledges, "the brakes of intelligence failed." There is emerging evidence of self-knowledge and a revelation of self-discovery in this admission.

and now I feel my great roots unearth, free and ...

This entry opens with Guevara reflecting on the moment in the journey where he realises that he is no longer all consumed with his love for Chichina. He reflected, "I still believed I loved her until this moment, when I realized I felt nothing." We also see the sensitive side of Guevara as the realisation is clearly quite traumatic for him and a moment worthy of noting in his diary.

Guevara is able to find solace in the natural landscape as they visit a lookout the next day in Chile. "It is a kind of crossroads: at least in that moment it was for me." In this discovery of self is a link to Romanticism. (Research the Romantic Movement if you have not studied it and consider the parallels.) As they depart Argentina for Chile, Guevara has reached a personal turning point and his new focus is Chile and what lies beyond for him. He recognises this while recalling the lines of the Otera Silva poem first mentioned in ... *lovesick pause* (p36).

objects of curiosity

The young men are objects of curiosity to the doctors they meet. They are a curious sight and they also impress them with knowledge of leprosy since leprosy was not as pressing a health issue in Chile. The young men showed interest in visiting the leper colony on distant Easter Island but at that stage they were still focussed on other, more selfish exploits as evidenced in the following quote, "In those happy days in the south of Chile, when our stomachs were still full and we were not yet totally brazen, we merely asked him for an introduction..." It seemed that he regretted not making more of an effort when help was offered to them.

The travellers discover Chilean hospitality and commented on, "exceedingly friendly people, (who) were warm and welcoming wherever we went."

Guevara learns how to drive a car – another new discovery told in an amusing tone.

Guevara also reflects on his discovery of the harbour and the merchandise which is different from back home in Argentina. He stated, "there was something indigenously American, untouched by the exoticism invading our pampas." (Pampas means their plains). Is this a discovery that indigenous culture has been better preserved in Chile than in his home country?

the experts

In this entry, Guevara and Granado continue to enjoy generous Chilean hospitality, this time from a young vet student.

Guevara includes an excerpt from the local paper as they entered an article about themselves. In the article, they are described as leprosy experts, which Guevara describes as, "the epitome of our audacity." He acknowledges their immaturity and possible lack of responsibility at this point in allowing everyone to think that they were experts in leprosy, while Guevara has not even finished his medical degree. Again, this is a valuable point to recall for comparison when charting the discoveries and changes within Guevara. While there is evidence of growing self-awareness at this stage in the text, there is still evidence of brash audacity and lack of concern for others.

Passing themselves off as "experts", at this point, is something that the two men discover to be to their advantage. As a result this is the first of many times that they employ this tactic.

the difficulties intensify

Problems with 'La Poderosa II' recur – this time a punctured tire, causes them to seek shelter for the night.

Due to their new found fame as "the Experts" the two travellers are treated "like kings". Guevara relented, "As usual, Chilean hospitality wiped us out."

When they continue, the motorbike's gearbox is smashed in a spill, and again they are offered generous hospitality, assistance and friendship. 'La Poderosa II' is becoming increasingly unreliable.

At the end of the diary entry, Guevara allows his moral judgement to be swayed by excess wine. His attempted indiscretion with one of the local married women results in the young men having to make a quick exit from a party, "pursued by a furious swarm of dancers." Self-discovery is therefore seen as not solely one directional. The men travel towards new values but not without backward glances and relapses as revealed through the events of the diary entries. Thus, discovery is seen not just as a product but a process.

la poderosa II's final tour

Problems with the bike continue and a serious accident is narrowly averted. Despite their efforts to fix it and despite the generous hospitality afforded to "the Experts", they reach the difficult decision to continue without the bike by the end of this diary entry.

Guevara shares some amusing toilet humour involving their host's sun-drying fruit, causing them to make another hasty retreat and confirming the earlier point that maturation is not without regression!

The decision to continue without the bike, however, is taken with an awareness of looming transportation difficulties. The quotation, "It was our last day as 'motorized bums'; the next stage seemed set to be more difficult as 'bums without wheels,'" serves to illustrate this point.

It is interesting that Guevara labels himself and Granado as "bums", another word for aimless wanderers living off the kindness of strangers and simply seeking adventure. Later, we witness his transformation through his discoveries to someone more purposeful. This label, when set against outcomes of the journey, serves to again elucidate the concept of self-discovery as a significant theme in the text.

The loss of 'La Poderosa II' is a significant turning point in the text so it is worth noting on any timeline or chronological map you might make of significant events.

firefighters, workers and other matters

This diary entry opens with the boys sleeping in a fire station in Chile for a few nights. Guevara comments on the frequency of fires in the region and believes a part of this may be due to the low socio-economic conditions of most of the people, including their lack of education and the use of poor quality building materials used in housing.

Guevara manages to find pleasure in the company of the three daughters at the fire station and the volunteers. He tells us about his new experience of being with the firefighters at an actual fire. He describes how Granado saved a cat for the owners, "receiving effusive congratulations for his unrivalled heroism." Guevara's use of hyperbole injects humour into his writing and responders continue to see he is a skilful, engaging writer.

The difficulties encountered with 'La Poderosa II' are eased by the connection with the firefighters and the distraction of the new experience. Guevara now describes the bike as "a corpse". He uses personification to emphasise the connection they felt with the bike and the significance of losing it.

Guevara then recounts the job they took as removalists. The story reveals continuation of a light-hearted and casual attitude towards the trip. Their confidence was so high that they refused the tiny sum of money offered to them in return. Guevara says they would definitely have taken it later in their trip. He says that they "took righteous offense" at the lack of generosity. This pride would be removed by the discoveries of their journey in the coming months. "If he'd offered it three months later, it would've been a different story." Such statements from the perspective of hindsight reveal clear evidence of changed attitudes, thus highlighting a process of discovery.

The boys awaited their visas to get into Peru and, in the meantime, met up with friends who were a part of a travelling water polo team. Once again, they have another night of Chilean hospitality which leaves them feeling far from vibrant.

The following day, an interesting incident occurs where Guevara and Granado are exploring the mountains and the water polo team are being led on a tour by members of the host polo club. Guevara describes the members of the polo team as being "embarrassed" as they initially seemed reluctant to admit that they knew the pair and introduce them to these "distinguished ladies of Chilean society". Here we witness the class divide, with Guevara and Granado being on a different side to the one they were born into, dressed as they were in their "unusual attire". He states that they were still "as friendly as people could be from worlds as different as theirs and ours at that particular moment in our lives."

This incident illustrates that the young men are continuing to mature, and that they are taking the superficial implications of their transformation in their stride. What affects them far more is the farewell to 'La Poderosa II', as tears drop down Granado's face.

The diary entry ends with Guevara once again reflecting on the beauty of nature and humorously commenting that the truck they were travelling in was carrying, "the heavy weight of us freeloaders." They are now homeless, without transport and relying almost entirely on the kindness of strangers for the most basic of human needs. It is in these times that they will make their most significant discoveries about themselves and the people they connect with along their journey.

la gioconda's smile

La Gioconda is the Spanish phrase for the Mona Lisa and the name of a cheap restaurant in Valparaiso. The young men frequent this restaurant during their stay, so the title of this diary entry may be referring to this as a positive experience in a time of new discovery. The smile of the Mona Lisa is enigmatic and this also links with the content of this entry. Rather than self confident and self assured, the travellers start to question the injustices in life and find, like attempts to explain the smile, a puzzling mystery.

"We had come to a new phase in our adventure" Guevara states, recognising a turning point in their trip. He describes their previous position as being one of upper class travellers who had wealth and position as identified through the metaphor, "knights of the road" and sustained allusion to high social status, seen in the term, "wandering aristocracy". It is significant that Guevara uses these terms as his way of thinking and viewing the world. His view changes from one of internal focus to one with greater awareness of class, especially as his status is about to change. He states that they had, "calling cards with our impeccable and impressive titles," but now they have lost their title of "the experts" and have to discover Latin America as, "shadows of our former aristocratic selves." Now they are "hitchhikers with backpacks". As self-acknowledged members of a lower social class, based on changed circumstances, their travelling experiences are, by necessity, different and now involve meeting their basic needs.

We see immediately how treatment of the travellers has changed. In Chile, they merely had to introduce themselves and they were, "treated like Kings." Here, the extent of the kindness is that they are allowed to sleep on parasite ridden wooden planks. Luckily, they are saved by their reputation, carried over from Chile, and escape the first-hand experience of poverty.

However, in this town, they do experience poverty second hand, witnessing it as they explore their surroundings. Guevara's description of their wanderings is full of imagery of the hopeless and sombre. The city is personified; "As it grew it clambered up the hills that sweep down to their deaths in the sea." He describes the discoveries they make along the way, "talking to the swarms of beggars," and how, "our distended nostrils inhale the poverty with sadistic intensity." These descriptions each serve to emphasise the plight of the people. The word "swarm" has connotations of bees, emphasising the insignificance of the people who are valued as insects only. It also emphasises the large number of people in this position. Likewise, in the second example, he describes how he "inhales the poverty'" suggesting that this discovery is becoming a part of his way of being, the oxygen that he is breathing in. It emphasises the depth with which he is taking on this discovery and allowing it to change the fundamental elements of his own person.

Guevara examines a woman with asthma. He attributes much of her medical condition to her living conditions as she breathes in the "acrid smell of concentrated sweat and dirty feet that filled her room, mixed with the dust of a couple of armchairs, the only luxury items in her house." He goes on to comment that, as a doctor, he feels an overwhelming sense of helplessness that there are people who are suffering in these conditions when there are other people who live luxurious lives by comparison (himself included). These are the moments of discovery that lead to his internal transformation. Unlike the overall journey, these epiphanies are sudden and unexpected:

"It is at times like this, when a doctor is conscious of his complete powerlessness that he longs for change: a change to prevent the injustice of the system."

Guevara's discoveries in meeting these people lead to him being confronted by his own helplessness in the face of this social inequality or unfairness. Social injustices and the internalising of such leads to changed values and attitudes for Guevara.

Guevara discusses the cycle of poverty that he feels powerless to change. Due to the woman's medical condition, she can no longer work as a waitress, resulting in the decline of her living conditions and the subsequent worsening of her medical condition. He also discusses the prejudice that is suffered by the lower class people, both at the hands of society and their own family members who are also struggling to survive.

"Individuals in poor families who can't pay their way become surrounded by an atmosphere of barely disguised acrimony; they stop being father, mother, sister or brother and become a purely negative factor in the struggle for life and, consequently, a source of bitterness for the healthy members of the community who resent their illness as if it were a personal insult to those who have supported them."

Guevara here has discovered something new. No doubt, he already knew about poverty throughout the continent and the social stigmas attached to it. However, through his encounter with this old woman, he has discovered how the sick, who have become sick as a result of their poverty, can be shunned and resented by their own family. For him this emphasises what he calls the, "profound tragedy" that impacts the lower classes, or as he describes them in Marxist terms, "the proletariat". This word choice is a clear indicator of how this discovery is impacting his political thinking as he turns to Marxist terminology to explain the situation.

This has been a significant incident for him as he continues to reflect on the futility of what he has witnessed. He is also starting to think about ways to make change and comments on how politicians can make a difference. This is the first time that we see Guevara make serious and passionate statements about how society needs to change, calling on politicians to make a difference. Here we, the responders, are starting to discover the change in Guevara. He concludes, "How long this present order, based on an absurd idea of caste, will last is not within my means to answer, but it's time that those who govern spent less time publicizing their own virtues and more money, much more money, funding socially useful works." This conclusion reflects his changed outward rather than inward, self-focussed thinking. Another example of how this incident impacts him is found in, "When I leave, I am followed by the fawning words of the old woman and the family's indifferent gaze." Here, he is actually unable to forget what he has seen as he has been changed by the experience. His focus changes from travel and self, to social justice and others.

The following incidents show insight into the relationship between the poorer people and the police. A woman does not report a very serious incident of violence where she describes a man slashing at another woman. He is described as "skinning her alive." Her reason for not reporting it to the police is because she doesn't trust them. She had reported things before and they told her she was crazy and threatened to lock her up. This is an example of police corruption as they turn away from the violence that impacts the lower classes, possibly as they have no financial gain from this. However, there is pay off for them in working with the wealthy, as the wealthy are more likely to give bribes and rewards. Such discovery results in challenges to Guevara's world view.

The travellers decide to go by ship to avoid the desert and its challenges. Guevara discusses the setbacks they face due to the bureaucracy of the system. No one seems particularly eager to help them, no doubt because of their "hobo appearance" as Guevara describes it. Whenever they apply through the official system to get work visas, they find their applications are rejected, presumably because of either prejudice due to their social status or indifference on behalf of the people working in the government jobs.

The young men decide that they will have to become stowaways to continue their journey. This leads them again to discover first-hand the experience of poverty and the necessity of committing a crime to survive.

stowaways

This diary entry opens with the travellers hiding in the toilet of a boat in order to continue their travels. There are some graphic descriptions associated with their location, told with good humour.

When they present themselves to the captain and he asks what they were thinking, Guevara confesses; "The truth is we hadn't thought through a thing", thus demonstrating that their improvisation, spontaneity and youthful naivety continues to be evident.

Despite this, and the fact that being found results in labour, they take time to enjoy nature and admire the ocean. By taking risks to gain new insights and adventures, they have been rewarded positively.

At this stage Guevara presents to his readers a discovery made about himself and his friend and their calling in life. "There we understood that our vocation, our true vocation, was to move for eternity along the roads and seas of the world."

this time, disaster

The next stowaway experience is not so positive, although it is told as a very amusing anecdote. While they are installed with tons of melons in a secure spot, they are unfortunately found due to eating too many of them, with melon skins "floating away Indian file on the tranquil sea."

They next decide to head towards Chile's famous copper mine, Chuquicamata, now the biggest open cut copper mine in the world. Along the way, they make friends with a married couple who are Chilean communists and who have suffered considerable hardships due to their beliefs. The man's "companeros" have been executed for their political crimes and "are said to be somewhere on the bottom of the sea."

Guevara is truly inspired by this couple. He describes them as, "the living representation of the proletariat in any part of the world." Guevara says that, in this moment, he felt renewed compassion for the human race, a discovery he made as a result of his meeting this man and his "starving wife" who gladly suffered to keep the hope of social justice alive. As this couple is committed to being communist and cannot find work anywhere else due to prejudice, they must go and work in the dangerous sulphur mines.

Guevara continues to reflect on the pair after they have parted, showing the responder the impact that discovering them had on him. He concludes, "it's a great pity that they repress people like this." He acknowledges that the government sees communists as vermin but he sees them as simply, "Longing for something better." Is this the beginning of a revolutionary Guevara?

Guevara's language changes as his resentment for the European bosses of the mines becomes evident. He describes them as, "the blond, efficient and arrogant managers," who only speak "primitive Spanish" and who ask the travellers not to take up too much of their time.

On a tour through the mine, they learn that the miners are striking for "a few more centavos", which is not a lot of money. However, the bosses are refusing to give it to them and, due to the strikes, are actually losing more money than the workers are asking for. Their guide sees this as a matter of principle as he believes the bosses are refusing to give them better conditions as they do not want to give up their power over the workers. The guide talks about his hope for a new government under General Ibanez.

The guide is surprised by Guevara and Granado's questions as they ask not only about how the mine works but about lives lost as a result of poor working conditions. Their humanity is contrasted with the inhumanity of the mine where "Cold efficiency and impotent resentment go hand in hand ..."

Once again, the discoveries of this journey have had a significant impact on Guevara who is coming to understand the rationale for communism and why people are turning to it for hope. He says he sees communism as, "a protest against persistent hunger transformed into a love for this strange doctrine."

As Guevara would go on to sacrifice his life for this doctrine (after the period of *The Motorcycle Diaries*), communing with these people and understanding their plight are important and life-changing discoveries for Guevara.

chuquicamata

Guevara uses a lot of powerful, harsh figurative language to describe the mine and its surroundings. An example is seen in, "a beauty without grace, imposing and glacial." He describes the mountains as displaying "their grey spine, prematurely aged in the battle with the elements, their wrinkles that do not correspond with their real geological age." This personification emphasises the harsh severity of the environment and links the landscape with the suffering and exploitation of the people who live and work there.

Further on, Guevara uses contrasting language to emphasise the differences between nature, which he loves, and the harsh machines of industry. He describes the mountains using the term, "brother," however, he describes the earth moving equipment as "soulless arms of the mechanical shovels". He draws attention to the many people who have died doing this work, using a metaphor so the audience will associate the machines with exploitation and human suffering. In this metaphor he describes how the machines are, "spiced as they would be with the inevitable human lives – the lives of the poor, unsung heroes of this battle who die miserably in one of the thousand traps set by nature to defend its treasures, when all they want is to earn their daily bread."

Guevara also uses powerful language here to emphasise the unfairness. The "traps set by nature" is a reference to the gasses that are omitted when the ground is disturbed in order to get the minerals, described as nature's "treasures". Guevara sees that nature is defending herself against the corporations that are extracting this treasure for their own profit. However, these defences of nature cause the death and suffering of the workers. They must work in order to eat ("earn their daily bread") but, in doing this work, they are the ones who die in the "thousand traps set by nature to defend its treasures." Guevara does not see nature as the enemy. He sees her as doing what is natural for her to do. However, the workers end up suffering. This could arguably be prevented if the corporations cared more for their workers. Guevara gives a detailed account of how mining works and creates strong imagery of the manufacturing process which includes the workers, whom he describes as "3, 000 souls", working to, "exploit the sulphate ore". Guevara resents both the exploitation of Nature, evident through his use of personification, and the exploitation of the workers. His use of "souls" is a powerful use of synecdoche and serves to highlight the physical exploitation of the workers and foreground their daily risk.

Guevara describes why the copper mines are so important to the Chilean government and concludes they are, "an essential component of various types of weapons of destruction." Guevara emphasises the role that politics and economics have to play in this "tragedy".

However, for Guevara, his focus is on the people and their suffering. He states, "it would do well not to forget the lesson taught by the graveyards of the mines, containing only a small share of the immense number of people devoured by cave-ins, the silica and the hellish climate of the mountain." The use of strong emotive words with references to death highlight Guevara's growing anger over the plight of the poor.

Exposure to the mine has led to more discoveries for Guevara about the different ways in which the governments of countries exploit their people and the ways in which people suffer as a result. He is becoming more and more passionate about this cause and increasingly committed. This is evident as we reflect on the beginning of the text and compare the Guevara who was full of wanderlust and a desire for adventure, with the Guevara of this section. The Guevara who is represented at this point in the text is driven by a concern for social injustices, is focussed on serious political issues and is narrating with a strong tone of sobriety.

arid land for miles and miles

In this diary entry, the young men, somewhat naively, set off to cross the desert on foot without a water bottle. They end up returning to the town and spending the night.

Remember the opening lines of *The Motorcycle Diaries*, where Guevara denies that this is a story of 'heroic feats'? In this diary entry, Guevara humbly admits that they are stupid, rather than heroic.

The young men overcome the challenging physical environment and mental exhaustion they are faced with. They connect with striking mine workers and join a football team which earns them food, board and transport to Iquique.

By the end of this diary entry, Guevara's tone is euphoric. He notes that "we saw from our vantage point the whole city rising to meet us."

the end of chile

On the next part of the journey, the travellers retrace the footsteps of one of the great Spanish Conquistadors (Conquerors) named Valdivia. Guevara discovers a new appreciation for the physical challenges he must have faced in trying to conquer this area (eg travelling 50 to 60 kilometres per day without discovering a drop of water).

In addition to Valdivia, Guevara also references Caesar who famously stated that he would rather be first man in a small village than the second man in Rome.

By drawing on Valdivia and Caesar, Guevara can be seen to appreciate the role of fierce determination and a drive for power, in the achievement of significant discoveries. Guevara concludes, "Valdivia's actions symbolize man's indefatigable thirst to take control of a place where he can exercise total authority."

While appreciating Valdivia's physical achievements, Guevara is critical of the means through which they were achieved. He identifies Valdivia's "craving for limitless power...so extreme that any suffering to achieve it seems natural..." Here a critical tone reveals discovery of self through the emergence of strong values and personal and political beliefs.

By contrast, Guevara has shown that he is not like Valdivia. He questions the suffering and exploitation he witnesses and reveals to the reader, through the diary entries, that he is strikingly more concerned with humanity than these conquerors in history proved themselves to be.

Guevara has started to refer to people more commonly by their political leanings (i.e. Communist) or by their economic place in society than he did at the beginning of his account. He refers to a doctor who, "showed us as much disrespect as an established, financially secure bourgeois can show to a couple of hobos." Guevara's subject of writing and language choices are changing as his identity changes as a result of his discoveries. The travellers then farewell Chile and move to Peru.

chile, a vision from afar

Guevara opens this diary entry with reflection on how his opinions have changed, just one year since writing his travelling notes. In order to stay true to the task at hand, he decides to reflect on his experiences at the time.

Guevara notes the poor health care in Chile. Then he made new discoveries revealing that it was not as bad as he originally thought.

He describes the inequality evident in the way different people were treated in regard to health care. If someone worked at the mine, it was considered that they were contributing to the system financially and so their access to health care was cheaper than someone who did not work in the mine. He notes the state of sanitisation in the hospitals was particularly poor with, "filthy operating rooms", "pitiful lighting" and a lack of adequate surgical instruments. He reflects on the various problems in Chile, including high unemployment, low wages, low standard of living and very little protection for the workers in terms of job security. He believes that it is because of these conditions, that many Chileans immigrate to Argentina for a better life. He laments the fact that, when he asked a manager at the copper mines about the loss of human life, the man just gave a "meaningful shrug". Recalling this event emphasises the sense of helplessness that is felt by the people.

Guevara moves on to the political scene with his analysis of the candidates for the approaching election and his reference to the communists being without the right to vote. Most revealing are his perspectives on the working class people, and the role of the United States. He sees that,"Chile as a country offers economic promise to any person disposed to work for it, so long as they don't belong to the proletariat." Additionally, he thinks the best thing for Chile to do is to, "shake its uncomfortable Yankee friend from its back," but he also recognises that, due to America having so much financial investment in the country, and therefore control, this is going to be very difficult.

These types of comments, which we have not seen expressed so clearly before, reflect the change in thinking that is occurring as a result of Guevara's discoveries. He is becoming more passionate about these causes as a result of seeing the poor conditions of the people directly.

Guevara's strong language choice reflects his newly discovered sense of injustice and indicates the beginning of the revolutionary who became Che Guevara. Che Guevara saw it as his calling in life to assist the proletariat and to take back power from corrupt governments. He died, aged 39, fighting for this cause.

tarata, the new world

This diary entry again highlights the physical hardship of travelling for Guevara and Granado. They have to walk in darkness in the cold desert and try to sleep by the side of the road. They have come a long way from the journey being about adventure and freedom and there is a distinct change in tone as the physical journey becomes harder and takes an emotional and mental toll on them. Clearly, Guevara's thoughts about life are continuing to extend to other people and their plight.

In this section, Guevara talks about how Argentina and Argentinians are seen as being the lucky people in Latin America. He claims when travelling, we often discover our national identity as we meet new people. The pair were received "like demigods" by local people who longed to hear stories from Argentina where, "the poor have as much as the rich and the Indian isn't exploited or treated as severely as he is in this country." Guevara begins to discover a strong sense of pride for his home country as he tells the working class people in the next few entries about life in Argentina.

We are introduced to the state of travel for the indigenous people. The travellers hitch a ride on one of these trucks and note, "As usual, it was transporting a cargo of human livestock, the most profitable business of all there." Because this is illegal, the people have to suffer in silence or risk criminal conviction. Once again, the wealthy, that is the trucking companies, are able to profit from the desperation of these working class people. Guevara and Granado would never have been able to witness this first hand if they did not embark on this trip that put them side by side with these people.

The entry ends with a description of the city of the Aymarans. Their experience with nature again seems to revive the travellers and as they entered Estaque, their, "ecstatic eyes fixed themselves momentarily on the landscape..." They find the landscape breath taking but are overcome by the impact that colonisation has had on the people. Guevara writes,

> *...the town's very breath evokes the time before Spanish colonization. But the people before us are not the same proud race that repeatedly rose up against Inca rule, forcing them to maintain a permanent army on their borders; these people who watch us walk through the streets of the town are a defeated race.*

This juxtaposition truly brings home to him the plight of the people. Guevara's reflections are very sombre and he emphasises the desperation and helplessness of the inhabitants in the following quote, "some give the impression they go on living only because it's a habit they cannot shake." This reflection reveals Guevara's profound change in thinking from superficial and self-focussed, to deeply empathetic.

in the dominions of pachamama

Again, the travellers find themselves in a truck that is taking human cargo in awful conditions. They are given special privileges as they are not Indians. They're given some wooden planks to sit on, "separating us from the foul-smelling and flea-ridden human flock below us, their potent but warm stink like a virtual lasso." The author uses a simile and animal imagery to emphasise the over powering smell and the degradation of the people.

Guevara shows respect for the "remarkable" indigenous people, the Indians, who were "treading through the snow, their bare calloused feet not seeming to worry them, while we felt our toes freeze in the intense cold, despite our boots and woolly socks." He uses a powerful simile, "At a weary, steady pace, they trotted along like Llamas in single file." The comparison of the people with native fauna both stresses the sense of connection to place and again dehumanises the people as they are likened to dumb animals who go where they are expected and grow acclimatised to conditions.

Guevara and Granado continue their journey, sharing stories with other travellers who are curious to hear about Argentina and the "wonderful land of Peron." Guevara is even asked for a copy of the constitution, and he "enthusiastically" agrees to send it to the man.

They meet another man who had been branded a criminal for his political beliefs. He had lost his job as a school teacher, for being a member of the APRA party (American Popular Revolutionary Alliance). Again, Guevara discovers someone who has tried to make positive change in his country and has suffered as a result, losing both his job and his freedom.

The man educates them about native Indian rituals and how, despite the Spanish trying to eradicate the culture of the native people, they were unsuccessful in completely destroying it in this region. This survival of traditional Indian culture is inspiring to Guevara.

Guevara records some of the comments made by the teacher about the treatment of his people, the Aymara race. Guevara is inspired by this man who grieves for, "the Indian's present condition, brutalized by modern civilisation and their companeros," because of their position, "between two worlds". This description emphasises the helplessness faced by these people as they struggle to belong with one side or the other. He continues to talk about practical ways in which he thinks the situation can be improved for the proletariat. He identifies, "the need to build schools that would orientate individuals within their own world, enable them to play a useful role within it." This is, however, precisely the reason why the government does not want to do this as to educate the lower class people would be to empower them and they would use that power to stop the government from exploiting them and making money from their ignorance. The government benefits far more from the current system of meagre education that "fills them with shame and resentment, rendering them unable to help their fellow Indians and at the severe disadvantage of having to fight within a hostile white society that refuses to accept them." The well-educated Guevara explains that the only hope for these people is that their children may go on to achieve the freedom and better life that they seek. For themselves, they feel powerless to make change.

Guevara is clearly impacted by his discovery of these people. He records conversations with them and sees encounters with them as significant moments in the journey. He is continuing to focus his notes more on the people and their social and political struggles rather than on the physical elements of the journey and funny anecdotes along the way. This change in selected content is evidence of the process of Discovery.

lake of the sun

This short entry is about the trip to the lake surrounding the bay Puno. Here the two men find that the checkpoint officers are less hospitable towards them. However, they use the opportunity to meet more of the local people and gain a better understanding of the native Indian people who have retained much of their traditional culture. Their interpreter tells them about some far off islands where the native people live entirely in the old culture as they have been isolated from the changes that were brought about with colonisation. He says that those people would have, "barely ever have seen a white man." Again, this fact raises questions regarding colonisation and discovery.

toward the navel of the world

The heading of this diary entry refers to the journey towards Cuzco, seen as the centre of the historic Inca Empire.

Guevara recalls an incident which shows the corruption of the police. When they go to the police station, the sergeant is clearly drunk and is keen to continue to party with Guevara and Granado, despite his responsibilities as an on-duty sergeant. The culture of the town and desensitisation to gun violence is evident when the sergeant is playing games using a loaded gun and is gambling with the young men. At one point, he shoots a hole in the wall.

The owner of the pub calls the police but finds that they refuse to help her as it would mean arresting their own sergeant. She is clearly aware that, by pushing the police into justice, she will only bring more trouble on herself. This is deduced from the words, "...but a quick mental calculation of the pros and cons was enough for her to keep her mouth shut." Therefore, the corruption of the police is evident as they choose to ignore the damage that has been done. The people cannot even rely on their police force for protection.

The prejudice against the local Indians is again seen as the boys travel in another truck towards their next destination. In the truck, there are some travellers from Lima who recognise Granado and Guevara as Argentinians and are keen to distinguish themselves from the local people due to their own sense of pride. "The whole time they tried to show us how much better they were than the silent Indians, who endured their taunts and showed no signs of being bothered."

They continue to travel northwards. Guevara recounts witnessing a funeral, "And so, poor old somebody or other crossed to his final resting place like this, pursued by the hate of his fellow villagers who on every street corner unburdened themselves of him in flooding words". The tone is quite depressed as, despite all of the traditional rituals being upheld, few people seem to genuinely care about the man who has died.

the navel

Cuzco is the navel, the centre of the Inca world. In this diary entry, Guevara conjures Cuzco from three different perspectives.

Firstly, there is the perspective of the Incas, a Cuzco "inviting you to become a warrior and to defend, club in hand, the freedom and the life of the Inca." Secondly, the perspective of "... a hesitant tourist, to pass over things superficially and relax into the beauty beneath a leaden winter sky." Thirdly, there is the perspective of the Spanish invaders, who displayed "formidable courage" in conquering the region in the name of Spain.

This is a thoughtful diary entry which captures in very few words, the beauty and complexity of Cuzco's history and culture. Guevara is discerning in his discovery of this unique city and the use of multiple perspectives is linked to new ways of thinking. This diary entry promotes the idea of discovery and rediscovery and exposes the social impact of discovery on the inhabitants of Cuzco.

the land of the incas

Guevara's description uses many emotive words and shows admiration and empathy for the Incas, while also emphasising the exploitation of the invading Spanish forces. He wrote,

> *When the white troops sacked the already defeated city, attacking the Inca temples with unbridled fury, they unified their greed for the gold that covered the walls in perfect representation of Inti the Sun God with the sadistic pleasure of exchanging for the bereaved idol of a joyful people, the joyful and life-giving symbol of a grieving people.*

Guevara, in highlighting the fact that the Spaniards built the Church of Santo Domingo above the walls of a grand Incan temple, highlights, "both lesson and punishment from the proud conqueror." Significantly and perhaps symbolically, the cathedral's cuppola (dome) has collapsed three times, but the

Incan foundations remain. Guevara confirms, "however colossal the disaster befalling its oppressor, not one of its huge rocks shifts from its place."

Guevara sees in these perfect stone structures, the "cry of the defeated warrior" and notwithstanding their outstanding workmanship, he implies the futility of their position when faced with the "impetuous actions of the white conquistadors."

Beyond Cuzco, Guevara notes other signs of the Incan past – notably Pisac, the fortress of Ollantaytambo and the famous Machu Picchu. For Guevara, Machu Pichu represents "the pure expression of the most powerful indigenous race in the Americas – untouched by a conquering civilization and full of immensely evocative treasures between its walls." He is clearly in awe of the Incas, and critical of the impact of the Spanish conquerors on this great people. Most tourists probably appreciate the architecture and/or the historical significance of the site. For Guevara, the site stirs his consciousness regarding the social impact of conquest and exploitation.

our lord of the earthquakes

Lord of the Earthquakes is a festival held on Easter Monday in Cuzco. A figure of Christ, known as Lord of the Earthquakes, is paraded through the town and people come out to pay their respects in a colourful procession.

Guevara notes a clear distinction between the lives of the Indians who have tried to keep their culture as pure as possible and the Indians who have given up their culture to become more European. He says that the native Indians, despite being at a

Catholic ceremony honouring a Christian God, have worn, "their best traditional costumes in expression of a culture of way of life which still holds on to living values."

When he sees the Indians who have adopted the European way of life, however, he sees the negative impact that this has had on them. He writes,

> *Their tired affected faces resemble an image of those Quechuas who refused to heed Manco II's call, pledging themselves to Pizarro and in the degradation of their defeat smothering the pride of an independent race.*

Manco II was an Incan leader at the time that the Spanish conquistadors came to conquer their lands. The conquistador at this time was known as Pizarro. Manco II managed to negotiate an agreement so that the Spanish could colonise the material wealth but he could still rule his people and they would keep their culture. However, it eventually turned to violence and conquest once the native Indians realised that the Spanish were exploiting them.

A third group of people is witnessed in the blond head of a North American, "a correspondent from another world lost amid the isolation of the Inca Empire." This implies that such tourists do not appreciate the deep history and culture of this place, and the wounds from conquest, which continue to resonate among the local indigenous people. There are several layers of discovery and some tourists from capitalist nations, unlike travellers who belong to that area, may not be able to reach the deepest layers.

homeland for the victor

This diary entry focuses on the decline of Cuzco, from being "the navel of the world", to "just another point on its periphery". Cuzco and its riches were discovered and then exploited by the Spanish and over a period of time, Lima became the new main city of Peru. Cuzco became "a relic of times gone by." For Guevara the reason to visit Cuzco is the city itself which "creates the impression of the peaceful, if sometimes disquieting, center of a civilization that has long since passed."

The imagery used by Guevara reflects his attitude towards the Incas and to the Spanish invaders. When he is describing the buildings of the Spanish, it is undertaken with very little favour. He uses a simile in one instance to highlight his disdain, "the cathedral seems to be decorated like an old woman with too much makeup." By contrast, his descriptions of Inca sites, such as Machu Picchu, in earlier entries, glorify the environment and the Inca civilisation.

cuzco straight

This diary entry also relates to Cuzco, but focusses more on the connections the young men made and their journey in and around the area, including a trip to Machu Picchu. They state regarding this time, "Our life in those two weeks never lost the hobo character which marked our whole journey."

Guevara recounts their connection with Dr Hermosa, Chilean swindlers, some more footballers and the passionate guide in the archaeological museum, who impacts them the most. This guide articulated a vision for helping Quechua people feel pride in their past, rather than simply shame in their present predicament.

Guevara takes pleasure in the fact that the curator with "eyes shining with enthusiasm and his faith in the future" is "proof of a race still fighting for its identity".

Specific references to discovery are made in this section regarding American archaeologist, Jeremy Bingham who 'discovered' the ruins of Machu Picchu in 1911. While Guevara does not go into this, Bingham's 'discovery' of the site has attracted controversy over the years due to the fact that he recovered thousands of artefacts and took them out of Peru, to Yale University. This is not unusual for archaeological findings of this era but can serve to emphasise the exploitation and loss that a discovery can lead to. On a larger scale, the discovery of one country by another, often results in loss rather than gain and this is a matter of perspective. Guevara's travels enlighten him and his discoveries relate to seeing with a new perspective and thus gaining new insights. In this way, knowledge is discovery.

Guevara described the train travel where essentially segregation was still practised. The third class was 'reserved' for the native Indians, meaning that the native Indians, no matter how wealthy, were not permitted to travel anywhere but the lowest class section of the train. Guevara describes the third class as being, "like cattle transport wagons", again likening their treatment to being like that of animals, only valued as a commodity, not as individuals. Guevara shares with his responders the dire results of a lack of education about hygiene. Since many of the native Indians knew nothing about basic hygiene, their personal habits were extremely unsanitary, no doubt leading to a lot of disease. He is quick to note that, "the tourists travelling in their comfortable rail coaches could only glean the vaguest idea of the conditions in which the Indians live, from the fast glimpses they catch as they speed past our train." Despite the tourists coming to discover and experience the native Indian culture, they are really only interested in seeing the sanitised, edited tourist version. They are not interested in finding out how the people really live. Guevara comments on how many simply fly in and fly out without getting this authentic experience. He has valued his experience of travelling amongst them and getting to know the people and this had led to important discoveries.

huambo

Guevara and Granado are keen to get to the leper colony at Huambo but are delayed because of lack of transportation. Food is scarce, they are a little bored, and Guevara has another asthma attack.

Guevara and Granado ask the lieutenant governor (village mayor) for some horses to take them to the leper colony. Two-thirds of the way along the difficult path to Huambo, they meet some Quechua people who tell them that the horses they were given were actually commandeered from them by the village mayor. They promptly returned the horses to their owners and continue on foot.

Guevara and Granado arrive at the leper colony where they discover another type of forgotten people. Guevara describes the leper colony and its inhabitants as "the condemned".

Guevara's description of the colony exposes his strong feelings about this place and the discoveries he will make here. He describes the sanitary conditions as "appalling" and "disastrous" and lambasts the "imbecility of the neighbouring locals" who further isolate the patients and the staff of the clinic by denying them hospitality and any reasonable assistance. Presumably the discrimination is due to the locals' ignorance about leprosy and how people contract it. Senor Montejo was not given a place to stay while he was setting up the clinic. In fact, "He had been forced to seek refuge in a pigsty, where he passed the night."

Guevara reflects on the fact that this discrimination suffered by individuals is also felt by the colony administrators who cannot get adequate funding to properly look after the patients and their nurses. Guevara describes the lack of appropriate laboratory and surgical equipment and includes the fact that the site is situated in a place infested with mosquitos.

Guevara and Granado decide to move on to get some treatment for Guevara's asthma and are accompanied by the same Quechua guide. In this class system, even the horse is relieved of the burden of carrying the luggage which is carried by the servant as the following quotation partly illustrates, "In the mentality of the district's rich people it's perfectly natural that the servant, although travelling on foot, should carry all the weight and discomfort." When Guevara and Granado take the bags for him, the guide's face is "enigmatic". This word means puzzled. This was an unusual gesture on the part of the travellers and the guide was perhaps uncertain what to make of their kindness.

ever northward

Guevara rests in hospital for a couple of days to recover. Hunger becomes a more consistent theme as they await transport to their next destination.

Guevara recounts two note-worthy incidents. The first is Granado's violent reaction to the discrimination they witness against an Indian woman who brought food for her husband in prison. He recorded, "His reaction must have seemed completely alien to the people who considered the Indians were no more than objects, who deserve to live, but only just." The generally accepted attitude towards the Indians continues to surprise the travellers. Guevara notes that after that incident they fell out of favour and needed to move on.

The second incident was when they were travelling in a truck and they, along with a local Indian boy, were meant to be keeping an eye on the cattle travelling with them. When Granado pointed out to the Indian boy that one of the cattle's eyes was being scratched by the horn of another, the Indian boy was indifferent. Guevara saw this as a significant moment. He saw the boy's response as representative of his whole race. "With a shrug of his shoulders, into which he poured the whole spirit of his race, he said, 'Why, when all it'll ever see is shit.'" The parallel highlights the apathy of a worn down people and emphasises the sense of helplessness and defeatism that the young men perceive in their young Indian travelling companion. His pessimistic attitude is probably a reflection of the poor conditions of his life so far where he feels that there is nothing in this world worth seeing, either for the cattle or presumably for himself. This incident embodies one of the main problems that Guevara discovers along his journey; not only are the native Indians treated as lesser people but they also do not seem to have hope that life can be any different.

through the center of peru

The hardships of the physical journey increase in this diary entry – this time the men's hunger is more extreme. They try many different things to distract themselves from it but they are struggling to shake what Guevara describes metaphorically as a "strange animal, living not just in one particular part but all over our bodies, making us nervous and bad tempered." They continue to travel in frightful conditions. Guevara and Granado are worried about the truck having an accident and this is a well-founded fear given all of the crucifixes on the road. However, their Indian travelling companions are so used to this perilous method of travel that they do not seem concerned at all.

Guevara briefly recalls another incident that reflects the prejudice of the local police towards the Indians. While conducting a murder investigation, they show the travellers a photo of an Indian man which they describe as, "the classic image of a murderer." They later warm to the man who reported the murder who lectures them on coffee, papaya and black slaves.

shattered hopes

The travellers believed they had accommodation in the next town but found themselves overstaying their welcome in the home of a distant acquaintance. They are duped into leaving as they're told that a truck has been organised to take them to Lima but they later discover that it would not even take them halfway. They managed to get another truck but the drivers also abandon them along the way.

Guevara outlines their "anniversary routine" step-by-step. This is a well-honed routine they use to obtain food and drink from hospitable people without expressly begging for it. Despite being strangers, they are still treated more hospitably than the local Indians.

As times become tougher, the young men have to beg for food. Guevara describes how he walked up to a hospital and asked for food. He reflects,"We were so brazen". This is a new feeling for them as they discover what it feels like to be ashamed. He comments, "Alberto was so ashamed he didn't even thank him." This experience gives the pair further insights into the daily struggle faced by poor people.

The dangerous journey continues – this time on board a truck driven by a man with poor eyesight. The driver considers himself lucky as his boss does not question him at all about his job as the boss only cares that the job is done (ie that he arrives at the destination). Readers find out that his driver's licence cost him a lot of money as he had to bribe the authorities to get it!

This type of travel is clearly dangerous – and the determination of this driver to keep driving despite the difficulties further underline the challenges faced by people on a daily basis. As the journey progresses and the diary entries increase, both the writer and readers discover more examples of the struggles of the poor and their lack of choices.

the city of the viceroys

Guevara sees their arrival in Lima as "the end of one of the most important stages in our journey". They have no money but are content. Lima was known by its Spanish conquistadors as the capital of the “viceroyalty of Peru” (hence the title of this diary entry).

Guevara records his appreciation of the cathedral in the city centre with its tall and graceful towers. Their favourite place was the Museum of Archaelogy and Anthropology, curated by an Indian scholar. They meet with Dr Hugo Pesce, expert leprologist who arranges accommodation for them at the leprosy hospital. They spend time at the hospital, at the museum and enjoying other cultural activities (a bullfight and a trip to the cinema). They are less impressed by the bullfight and the cinema.

For the two friends and travellers, the experiences which they continue to find most meaningful are those involving connections with people. One of the highlights for the young men is the farewell given by the leprosy patients when they depart Lima. They reflect, “If there’s anything that will make us seriously dedicate ourselves to leprosy, it will be the affection shown to us by all the sick we’ve met along the way.”

Guevara makes an interesting observation about “the many parts that make up our journey”. He includes, “furthering our knowledge” (through visits to museums and libraries) and from a scientific perspective (leprosy in particular) and the connection with Dr Pesce. This observation is interesting because it explicitly unpacks their journey of discovery through self education.

In terms of political observations, Guevara comments on Lima as “the perfect example of a Peru which has not developed beyond the feudal conditions of a colony” and he concludes that it “still waits for the blood of a truly emancipating revolution.” This symbol again reflects his use of imagery to emphasise his passion for revolution. The blood of revolution can be synonymous with freedom from oppression.

After departing from Lima they encounter more challenges on their physical journey – including further issues involving transport and health. Guevara's asthma is getting worse as they struggle to find appropriate treatment for him in the poorer areas they're visiting and with their minimal funds.

They are now aiming for Iquitos and continue to think creatively and connect with people to work towards that objective.

down the ucayali

This diary entry begins with the young men travelling by boat, in the first class section (for the rate of third class). Granado joined in the gambling on deck and won ninety soles (having put down only one sol at the outset).

Guevara's asthma worsened and the conditions on the boat, despite being first class, are not comfortable with aggressive mosquitos attacking them. Guevara looks out dreamily to the jungle, noting that "virgin forests are so compelling for spirits like ours that physical impediments and all the nascent forces of nature only served to stimulate my desire."

Guevara reflects on the class discrimination on the boat as they both find themselves somewhat shunned due to their appearance. He comments, "We were drawn more to the simple sailors than to that small middle class which, whether rich or not, is too attached to the memory of what it once was to allow themselves the luxury of associating with two penniless travellers." He says that, "the small victories they have achieved in life have gone to their heads." This is clearly an attitude that is not confined to the boat and his discovery further cements his own impression of the region and the social discrimination that occurs. The journey continues slowly and uneventfully apart from Guevara's worsening asthma.

When they finally arrive in Iquitos, they go directly to the International Cooperation Service. The doctor they search for is not in Iquitos, but they are welcomed with a hospital bed and food. After that they are back on board, with the mosquitoes, en route to San Pablo leprosy colony.

dear papi

This is the second letter back home which Guevara includes in his diary (this one to his father). In it he refers to their upcoming decisions about mode of travel, and focuses on his experience connecting with leprosy patients. He admits that, even though he finds leprosy interesting, he is not sure if it will hold his interest long term.

He shares with his father his discoveries about how treating people with respect can really have a significant impact on them. He describes how they shook hands with the leprosy patients without wearing gloves and spent time with them, treating them as normal human beings. He explained, "It may all seem like pointless bravado, but the psychological lift it gives these poor people – treating them as normal human beings instead of animals as they are used to – is incalculable and the risk to us, extremely unlikely."

the san pablo leper colony

In this diary entry, Guevara introduces us to the San Pablo leper colony, where 600 sick people live independently in jungle huts.

The conditions are much the same as the previous colony they visited, particularly for the healthy who work there. He tells us that it is "lacking basic amenities" including electricity and laboratory equipment.

They do rounds in the mornings with Dr Bresciani and learn about the type of leprosy which attacks the nervous system.

There is also time to fish, play chess and chat with others resident in the community.

saint guevara's day

On this day, it is Guevara's 24th birthday and a party is thrown for him. They enjoy the Peruvian national drink, pisco, and Guevara notes drily that, "Alberto is quite experienced regarding its effects on the central nervous system".

Guevara makes a speech which includes some political elements. This is possibly his first political speech to a large crowd of people. (Ultimately, he gives many speeches to inspire revolutionaries and he speaks at the United Nations for his cause.) After thanking his guests for their hospitality, he shares a key discovery of this journey. He states that, "after this journey more firmly than ever," they have they discovered that the division of Latin America into separate nations is "completely fictional" and that "We constitute a single mestizo race, which from Mexico to the Magellan Straits bears notable ethnographic similarities."

This is a very significant moment in this text and one worth discussing as an example of how Guevara's discoveries have shaped his identity. The use of the inclusive, collective pronoun "we" makes this a significant personal discovery. The title of the entry foreshadows his devotion to the newly discovered cause and highlights a changed motivation as Guevara considers others above self.

The next day, they visit a tribe of Indians. Guevara makes observations about their way of living which fascinates him. He also notes that the elderly seem to have less vitamin deficiency than the elderly in more developed areas of the jungle.

They spend their time assisting in the hospital and exploring their surroundings. They fish, play football and Guevara even swims across the Amazon in a two hour journey. The next part of the diary entry describes their preparations for the upcoming journey by raft on the *Mambo-Tango*.

When they leave, they are given a farewell performance by many of the patients and staff, again showing their appreciation towards Guevara and Granado.

debut for the little kontiki

This very short diary entry contains Guevara's reflections on the physical hardships of travelling on water. They suffer exhaustion and hunger and struggle to effectively manoeuvre their raft.

Guevara uses narrative devices to emphasise the challenges they are facing. He admits, "A morbid fatigue and an uneasy exhaustion overwhelmed me". The words "morbid" and "uneasy" emphasise his feelings of being in a survival situation where he feels vulnerable and helpless.

The writer does show optimism at these times, however, perhaps reflecting his growing maturity and confidence in dealing with the unexpected along the journey. He describes how he, "clung to the thought that no matter how bad things became, there was no reason to suppose we couldn't handle it."

dear mama

In this entry, Guevara writes to his mother from Bogota, Colombia.

He tells her about the Pan-American speech he gave at his birthday party, which won "great applause from the notable, and notably drunk, audience." The most interesting experience of the trip was the farewell by the leprosy patients who serenaded them on the jetty and gave speeches, together with Alberto's impressive speech that had the patients in fits of laughter.

He tells his mother about the beauty of their surroundings and the challenges and fears faced when travelling by raft. For example, when one of the hens they later planned to eat fell into the river,

> *The man who had swum the full width of the river in San Pablo didn't have the courage to dive in after it...' due to a fear of alligators they had spotted and a fear of water at night.*

The young men are able to connect easily with people they meet. An example in this diary entry is when they were asked to coach a football team, "while waiting for a plane". They are able to transform the weakest team into the runners-up. Guevara causes a violent reaction by bending down to wipe blood off his knee during the Colombian national anthem. Interestingly, Guevara was about to shout back, when he remembered "...our journey, etc.," and bit his tongue. In other words, the journey was more important than defending himself over an insignificant affront.

On arrival in Bogota they find accommodation on the university campus. Their growing political inclinations are also shown in their shunning of hostel accommodation. Guevara confirms,

> *We're not terribly poor but explorers with our history and stature would rather die than pay for the bourgeois comfort of a hostel.*

This type of thinking is in contrast to the start of their journey. Towards the end of their journey, the references to "our history and stature" indicate the journey has involved a process of discovery.

They are both offered jobs but after an altercation with the police, they decide to continue onto Venezuela.

When describing Colombia, Guevara shares his discovery that there is more repression than other countries they have been to. He senses that "the atmosphere is tense and it seems a revolution may be brewing."

This excites Guevara as he is witnessing the beginning of a social revolution, something that he will go on to make his life passion. He describes how the revolution comes from the people, that the countryside "is in open revolt" and that the military are unable to control them. He describes how the conservatives are unable to agree on a course of action and it seems to be quite dangerous and "suffocating". They decide to leave and head for Caracas.

on the road to caracas

Guevara opens this diary entry with a recount of the continued discrimination that they experience by people in authority such as police and customs. These people in power display a "spiteful insolence" and deploy intimidating tactics. Guevara resents this highly but understands that he has to co-operate to a certain extent if he wants to enter Caracas.

Guevara and Granado are reluctant to be exploited by a travel company who deny them the ability to travel in the cheapest way possible. In the end, however, they have to give in as Guevara's asthma gets worse. The travel conditions are unsafe, uncomfortable and interrupted by several problems with their transport such as flat tyres, punctures and faulty wiring. They can't sleep due to being crammed in. The driver continued for two days without sleep. This again reflects the unsafe working conditions of the people who are exploited.

On arrival in Caracas, Guevara gets an adrenalin injection for his asthma and "slept like a tiger".

this strange twentieth century

This diary opens with Guevara reflecting on how he feels about the trip as he is about to return home to complete his medical degree.

Guevara comments specifically on the close friendship and bond he has with Granado. He notes that they have become very close after spending many months, "side by side, through good and bad, accustomed to dreaming similar dreams in similar situations..." and he knows he will feel "Alberto's absence sharply".

Guevara gives some description of Caracas and the social conditions there. He describes how this is more of a multicultural area with African and Portuguese people. He says that, "Discrimination and poverty unite them in the daily fight for survival but their different ways of approaching life separate them completely." Their life together is "fraught with bickering and struggles." He experiences the division first hand when, after an incident, some African children hurl an insult towards him with "the height of contempt: 'Portuguese'".

Guevara visits some of the homes of the poorest African people and describes the awful living conditions there. He describes how transport containers are used as homes by the Portuguese. Interestingly, despite their squalid living conditions, they have luxuries such as electricity, refrigerators, radios and cars.

a note in the margin

Guevara opens his final diary entry with an ambiguous, dream-like narrative where he is admiring the stars and nature until a face appears. This man seems to have an impact on Guevara that no one else has had before. Guevara describes this moment as revelatory. While Guevara has heard similar "arguments" before, they did not make such an impression on him. The man has met with violence and travelled the world, experiences which Guevara admires and finds intriguing.

Just as they are about to part, the man starts talking about the power of the people. He says to Guevara:

The future belongs to the people, and gradually, or in one strike, they will take power here and in every country.

He talks about the importance of education and the challenge that they cannot educate themselves until after they take power. This paradox strongly suggests that other educated people who are connected to them need to assist them in realising that they need to fight for their independence.

The inspiring visitation makes some insightful predictions as to how he and Guevara will make "great sacrifices". He states that revolution will take the lives of many people and that Guevara will die, "with a clenched fist and a tense jaw, the epitome of hatred and struggle, because you are not a symbol (some inanimate for example) but a genuine member of the society to be destroyed; the spirit of the beehive speaks through your mouth and motivates your actions."

This enigmatic character accurately predicted that Guevara would die violently after many years of struggling to improve the conditions of the people. He also recognises that Guevara will be very useful in the campaign.

Guevara has an epiphany or a revelation about who he really is. His identity has changed as a result of this journey and he discovered what he wanted to dedicate his life to. He states, "I now knew...I knew that when the great guiding spirit cleaves humanity into two antagonistic halves, I would be with the people." He has discovered that his allegiance is with the working class people, not the colonists, not the capitalists, not the corporations.

He also speaks passionately for the first time about the fact that he will partake in violent revolution as he does not see peaceful protest as being effective.

I...howling like one possessed, will assault the barricades or the trenches, will take my blood-stained weapon and, consumed with fury, slaughter any enemy who falls into my hands.

His anger towards the injustice and his discovered passion for the cause is clearly evident in his emotive language. His description of himself being like an animal is evident in phrases such as, "howling like one possessed" and later, "I feel my nostrils dilate." He does not see any need to control his fury and passion for the cause and is willing to murder and transform into a wild beast to liberate those whom he has witnessed suffering.

He finishes the text with a rousing proclamation which draws on religious and war-like references, and incorporates symbolism which shows his utter dedication to the proletariat and his commitment to fight for their cause, even to matrydom. "I steel my body, ready to do battle, and prepare myself to be a sacred space within which the bestial howl of the triumphant proletariat can resound with new energy and new hope."

Think back to the diary entries at the beginning of the text. You can see that now, as a result of his physical journey and the journey of discovery, Guevara clearly knows what he wants to dedicate his life to. At the beginning, his desire is much more general – to explore Latin America. It is also self-focussed, to experience freedom, through adventure, for one who has a restless spirit. His political views have also sharpened throughout the journey and, by the end, he is dedicating himself, with religious zeal and with "new energy and new hope" to the proletariat.

As a result of these social and political discoveries, he will later be known as 'Che Guevara', the Latin American liberator who fights for the proletariat, sees himself as a Communist and whose life was sacrificed for the cause.

Che Guevara's later experiences are recorded in separate diaries (see the list at the end of *The Motorcycle Diaries*).

Appendix: Speech to Medical Students - a child of my environment

This appendix is a speech given by Guevara to Cuban medical students some eight years after writing *The Motorcycle Diaries*. It encourages the medical students to engage with their potential role in the revolutionary movement and it also informs the reader about what Guevara did next and how he continued to evolve as a revolutionary. Note this appendix is useful to students as Guevara reflects on his discoveries. Structurally, it forms a significant part of the text. Do not ignore it.

The introduction to the speech explains that Guevara is now a key figure in Cuba's revolutionary movement. By now, he has travelled around Latin America a second time with Granado. He recounts that his previous desires to make a difference would also involve "a personal triumph" and he admits he was "a child of my environment" in highlighting his individual role and desire for recognition.

He explains that their way of travelling through Latin America brought them into "close contact with poverty, with hunger, with disease, with the inability to cure a child because of a lack of resources, with the numbness..." that comes after the "hard-hit" classes are battered beyond a certain point. At this point, Guevara began to look into being a "revolutionary doctor".

After the 1954 coup in Guatemala, Guevara further developed this understanding – that individual effort is "naught": "A revolution needs what we have in Cuba: an entire people mobilized, who have learned the use of arms and the practise of combative unity, who know what a weapon is worth and what the people's unity is worth."

Next he shares that a revolutionary doctor is "a person who puts the technical knowledge of his profession at the service of the revolution and of the people."

He talks about the differences a new Cuba will offer – addressing poverty, hunger and education for all. He then seeks to orient the medical students' creative talent towards "social medicine", which he explains involves the task of

> *training and nourishing the children, the task of educating the army, the task of...redistributing the lands among those who previously did not reap the fruit of their hard work.*

Guevara talks about the need for individualism to disappear or rather for individualism in the future to be "the proper utilization of the whole individual, to the absolute benefit of the community." He states, "The doctor, the medical worker, should ... go to the heart of their new work, which is a person among the masses, a person within the community."

Guevara reflects on the experience of the first part of the Cuban revolution (on board the *Granma* and later in the Sierra Maestra) and encourages the doctors to seek the "prized treasure, the people's gratitude."

He claims there is a need for a move from 'charity' to 'solidarity' with the people: "We should go with an investigative zeal and with a humble spirit, to learn from the great source of wisdom that is the people."

Guevara states that the United States is the "enemy of all Latin America".

The end of the speech is a call to action, noting that the journey is ongoing:

> *...if we know the goals, if we know the enemy, and if we know the direction in which we have to travel, then the only thing left for us is to know the daily stretch of the road and to take it. Nobody can point out that stretch; that stretch is the personal road of each individual...*

PLOT QUESTIONS AND ACTIVITIES

- How would you describe Granado and Guevara at the beginning of the journey?
- What reasons do they give initially for wanting to travel? Do you think their reasons change along the way? If so, how and why?
- Identify five key discoveries they make along their journey.
- Do you think Guevara's experiences are significantly different from Alberto Granado's? Give reasons why or why not.
- Brainstorm all the discoveries the young men make along the way. Organise them into categories such as physical discoveries (about the environment or their own physical selves); discoveries about others and inner discoveries about themselves. You may also come up with other categories you feel are important.
- Using your brainstorming above, choose two to three per category which you think are most significant. Take notes on them and find quotes to support your ideas.
- Initially, there are very few inner discoveries made by the travellers. Why do you think they discover more significant things as their journey progresses?
- How do Guevara's discoveries impact his future and his identity?

CHARACTER ANALYSIS

Ernesto 'Che' Guevara

The main character in this text and its author is Ernesto Guevara. When the diary entries begin, he is a young, carefree medical student who is looking to travel for inspiration. He describes himself as "having the spirit of a dreamer" who has become "jaded" and wishes to seek adventure.

His adventures initially focus on enjoying life in a very superficial manner. Both he and Granado seem to be only interested in feasting, drinking to excess and enjoying the company of women.

The beginning of their journey is quite easy for them in terms of the travelling conditions. They are often, "treated like Kings" and Guevara regularly recounts the Chilean hospitality they enjoy with grateful admiration.

Guevara is a skilled writer and shares his love of nature with the reader in several diary entries. For example, "The tremor of nature cut straight to our hearts" (see summary for 'circular exploration')

While they begin the journey with some naivety, they regularly use improvisation, innovation and their people skills to overcome the challenges – as Guevara writes to his mother, they used their "usual resourcefulness to solve the thousand problems that plagued us along the way."

They begin to discover more about themselves when the journey becomes more physically difficult. Once their motorbike breaks down, they have to rely on the kindness of strangers, some of whom they take advantage of, for food and accommodation.

Part way into the journey, Guevara begins to appreciate that you can experience a deeper appreciation of the spirit of a place, if you can stay for a few days. From this point on, Guevara begins to witness and then experience poverty and exploitation more sharply.

At their lowest points, they are forced to sleep in the open and beg for food. They experience and can better understand hunger, poverty, sickness and the poor working conditions these people live with. Without this change in their journey, it is doubtful that they would have experienced the degree of hardship suffered by these people which, in turn, led to self-discoveries.

In the diary entry headed 'la giaconda's smile', Guevara notes his powerlessness and his longing for change in, "a change to prevent the injustice of the system". From here on Guevara becomes more focussed on other people and their plight and less concerned about himself.

The events in the diaries which most impact Guevara involve the leprosy patients who shower them with gratitude for treating them as normal human beings. Guevara and Granado are counter-cultural in many ways in the way they relate to people. This is especially notable in their approach to leprosy patients and in their reactions to discrimination and injustice.

This text is often described as a "coming of age" or a "bildungsroman" text as we witness Guevara change from being superficial and immature to someone who dedicates his life passionately to the cause of liberating those whom he sees as the most mistreated people.

Alberto Granado

As Guevara's travelling companion, we also hear about Alberto Granado throughout the text.

Granado is a likeable character who often spins the truth in order to assist their journey. He is a born story-teller, and is engaging and entertaining.

Guevara talks of Granado with much affection throughout the text. At the outset he mentions that this is a snapshot of "two lives running parallel for a time, with similar hopes and convergent dreams."

By the end when they have gone their separate ways for a time, Guevara misses Granado "so sharply."

Other characters

The other characters in the text are significant only for what they can teach Guevara or for what he discovers as a result of meeting them. These characters include: his girlfriend Chichina ('a lovesick pause' at the beginning) and the the Communist married couple from Chile. They met this couple on their way to the mines and they inspire him in the way that they have sacrificed comfortable lives by staying true to their beliefs. He describes them as, "a living representation of the proletariat"

Additionally, the school teacher from Puno (*in the dominions of pachamama*) who spent time in prison for his beliefs, is significant. Guevara learns a lot from him as he discusses what he feels should be done to improve the conditions of the proletariat. "In the convulsive clenching of his fist, one could perceive the confession of a man tormented by his own misfortune."

Likewise, the mestizo curator of the museum in Cuzco who speaks passionately about the plight of the Latin American people inspires Guevara. He suggests practical ways they can be helped. Guevara describes him as, "one more treasure of the museum" and "proof of a race still fighting for its identity."

There are many characters Guevara meets along the way and who shape him in unique ways. However, the characters listed above are worth gathering evidence on, in order to discuss in detail.

Guevara is not only shaped by people but also by his experiences. It is worth looking into some of these individual experiences as moments of significant discovery.

THEMATIC CONCERNS; TYPES OF DISCOVERY

Physical Discovery

As a result of the physical journey that Guevara and Granado undertake, there are many physical discoveries that occur. Obviously this is the most basic form of discovery that you would talk about and you are most likely to talk about the physical discoveries in terms of what they teach Guevara about himself rather than just discovery for discovery's sake. As they travelled the two men encountered new places and people, they discovered much about the countries and the people they encountered. They discovered more about the effects of colonisation on nations and saw first hand the beauty and destruction of nature at the hands of capitalism.

Discovery and appreciation of nature

There are several entries which show the young men's appreciation of nature. See for example, the diary entries headed, 'san martin de los andes', 'circular exploration' and 'on the seven lakes road'.

Natural beauty in 'san martin de los andes' helps them to realise that travelling is their 'destiny'.

In 'circular exploration', Guevara notes that "The tremor of nature cut straight to our hearts. We walked slowly so as not to disturb the peace of the wild sanctuary with which we were now communing."

In 'on the seven lakes road', Guevara records "the scent of wilderness caressing our nostrils."

At times the beauty of nature is able to distract them from the physical hardship they encounter. They discover their romantic sensibility as they come to appreciate nature.

Discovery through Physical Journey

This relates to the first topic, listed above. The physical journey undertaken by the young men over the nine month period is difficult but rewarding. When you mark the journey on a map, you will also see how significant their efforts were.

Physical experience is highly valuable and below are some points you might like to make about the physical discoveries made along the journey.

The nature of their physical travel changes throughout the text, resulting in personal challenges and other types of discovery. When in Chile, the boys find travelling to be quite enjoyable, easily finding accommodation, free food and drink and recounting humorous anecdotes of their travels.

As they lose the motorbike and head into poorer areas, they find that their experience of travel changes. They now must travel as the very poor do, on foot, by truck, raft or train. This type of travel presents more physical challenges for them, including hunger, thirst and the inability to sleep. However, travelling alongside the poorest people in Latin America also presents opportunities for new types of discovery.

Guevara would have been aware at the start of the text that discrimination and exploitation occurred in South America. However, it was not until he physically visited the mines and spent time amongst the lowest class, that the scale of the exploitation and discrimination became clear to him.

When Guevara tried to help the woman who was very sick with asthma (in 'la giaconda's smile'), the physical experiene of her living conditions and medical condition leads to the inner realisation that it is "when a doctor is conscious of his complete powerlessness that he longs for change: a change to prevent the injustice of the system."

The physical journey helps them appreciate their Latin American heritage. For example the journey in Peru to Cusco and then Machu Pichu and surrounding areas is significant in helping them appreciate the achievements of the Incas. Machu Pichu symbolises for Guevara, "the pure expression of the most powerful race in the Americas – untouched by a conquering civilization and full of immensely evocative treasures between its walls."

When travelling in Lima, a physical journey also leads to greater understanding of the plight of the Indian people. Travelling on a truck with livestock, the Indian boy minding them is indifferent when the horn of one cattle is scratching the eye of another. The boy shrugged his shoulders "into which he poured the whole spirit of his race" and said, "Why, when all it'll ever see is shit." On this physical journey, Guevara is able to perceive the sense of helplessness and defeatism of the Indian race.

By the end of *The Motorcycle Diaries*, Guevara is convinced by his travels that there is a "single mestizo race" and a united Latin America. This is a result of the physical experience of meeting Latin American people who share common traits.

Throughout the physical journey, the young men actively seek out knowledge from their connection with people, and their visits to museums and libraries. This leads to self-discovery.

Self Discovery

Many of the self-discoveries that Guevara experienced were a result of the physical journey and the social discoveries regarding injustices described in *The Motorcycle Diaries*. Therefore, there may be times where your analysis overlaps or you feel you may be repeating yourself. Practice responses and feedback from your teacher will be helpful for you to refine your writing technique. Remember to look back over the rubric.

Self to other-focus

Guevara changed his attitude and his perspective on life as a result of the discoveries he made about Latin America and himself. At the beginning of the text, he is self-focused — he enjoys food, alcohol, his girlfriend and generally his own freedom and pleasure.

However, by the end of the text, he talks about this less and less and instead focusses on what he can offer the people of Latin America. He matures as a result of his discoveries and becomes more outward looking and humble in his approach to life.

Again the speech given in the appendix is insightful in highlighting Guevara's journey away from individualism towards cooperation for the common good.

Affinity and connection with local people

The young men experience generous hospitality on their journey and have countless experiences connecting with local people – eating with them, chatting with them, playing football or travelling with them.

While Guevara comes from a privileged background and is a medical student, he increasingly finds the encounters with down-to-earth people more meaningful.

He highlights his encounters with leprosy patients as very special, and the farewells given to him by the patients are very memorable and significant for Guevara. He cites the farewell from the San Pablo leper colony (being serenaded on the jetty) as the most interesting experience of the trip. In a letter home to his father, Guevara notes how treating the leprosy patients with respect can have a significant impact on them. The usual approach is to teach them like animals so their approach is counter-cultural.

As "hobos", they find themselves increasingly isolated by middle class acquaintances and travelling first class on board a boat, they find themselves "drawn more to the simple sailors than to that small middle class..."

In the appendix, Guevara's speech given several years after the period of *The Motorcycle Diaries* encourages the medical students to "learn from the great source of wisdom that is the people." That is essentially what Guevara and Granado did during their travels.

Political awakening

Throughout the text, Guevara becomes increasingly attracted by communist fellow-travellers. He starts out as 'left-leaning' but by the end this has crystallised into a desire to achieve a revolution together with the proletariat.

By the end of the text, he perceives "a single Mestizo race". He no longer sees his identity as an Argentinian but rather as a Latin American. In his birthday speech, he talks about the importance of uniting the Latin American people in order to fight against oppression and improve their way of life. This self-discovery leads to a change in direction for Guevara from a young trainee doctor interested in leprosy to someone "ready to do battle" and to assist the "triumphant proletariat" to "resound with new energy and new hope."

Guevara changed his attitude and his perspective on life as a result of the discoveries he made about Latin America and himself. At the beginning of the text, he is self-focussed. He enjoys food, alcohol, his girlfriend and generally his own freedom and pleasure. However, by the end of the text, he talks about this less and less and instead focusses on what he can offer the people of Latin America. He matures as a result of his discoveries and becomes more outward looking and humble in his approach to life.

Guevara's identity fundamentally changes throughout this text. He discovers a deep connection with Latin American people (not just his fellow Argentinians), a growing political response to poverty and exploitation (seen in his attraction to communist travellers) and a sense that by the end, the journey is more important than himself.

Responders' discoveries

The text opens with the discoveries made by Guevara's daughter. She learns more about her father which also impacts her own identity (see analysis for more information).

Through engaging with this text, responders learn more about Guevara and how he came to be the inspirational revolutionary for the people of Latin America. This in turn can inspire self-discovery within responders.

LANGUAGE

Narrative Devices

Despite this being a non-fiction text, Guevara uses narrative elements which you may recognise from the fiction texts you have studied in the past. These techniques increase the engagement for the reader and emphasise emotions, images and experiences.

In the analysis section of this book, various techniques have been identified and their effect discussed. Guevara uses imagery, such as metaphor and personification. He also uses symbolism, repetition and emotive language to convey his ideas.

These techniques should be identified and discussed throughout your essay response and linked to the concept of Discovery.

Other non-fiction elements; Letters, photos, maps

Guevara writes and includes three letters in his text, two to his mother and one to his father. This technique emphasises the non-fiction nature of the text and adds authenticity.

Non-fiction elements such as photos and maps are included which also add authenticity to the text. These are also helpful for the audience as they can help readers follow the journey and connect with Guevara, Granado and their experiences.

Questions on Language

- Identify some examples of imagery used by Guevara. Why does he use metaphors? What is the effect?

- What symbols are used regularly throughout his entries? What is the effect of these symbols?

- In what ways is the bike, 'La Poderosa II', shaped through language to be like another character?

- Guevara's language changes throughout the text, becoming more emotive and passionate. Find examples of this and explain what this reflects about Guevara's character.

- Discuss how Guevara uses a mix of non-fiction and narrative elements to shape the audience's experience of his journey.

THE ESSAY

The essay has been the subject of numerous texts and you should have the basic form well in hand. As teachers, the point we would emphasise would be to link the paragraphs both to each other and back to your argument (which should directly respond to the question). Of course, ensure your argument is logical and sustained.

Make sure you use specific examples and that your quotes are accurate. To ensure that you respond to the question make sure you plan carefully and are sure what relevant point each paragraph is making. Topic sentences are helpful to begin each paragraph and it is solid technique to actually 'tie up' each paragraph by linking it to the question.

When composing an essay the basic conventions of the form are:

- Address the question, state your argument, outline the points to be addressed and perhaps have a brief definition.

↓

A solid structure for each paragraph is:

- Topic sentence (*the main idea and its link to the previous paragraph/ argument*)
- Explanation/ discussion of the point including links between texts if applicable.
- Detailed evidence (*Close textual reference- quotes, incidents and technique discussion.*)
- Tie up by restating the point's relevance to argument/ question

↓

- Summary of points
- Final sentence that restates your argument

As well as this basic structure you will need to focus on:

Audience – for the essay the audience must be considered formal unless specifically stated otherwise. Therefore, your language must reflect the audience. This gives you the opportunity to use the jargon and vocabulary that you have learnt in English. For the audience ensure your introduction is clear and has impact. Avoid slang or colloquial language including contractions (doesn't, eg, etc).

Purpose – the purpose of the essay is to answer the question given. The examiner evaluates how well you can make an argument and understand the module's issues and its text(s). In the case of the Area of Study, markers look for a deep conceptual understanding and you must reveal understanding using examples from your prescribed text and a related text or texts. An essay is solidly structured so its composer can present ideas with clarity. This is where you earn marks. Essays do not retell the story of a text or state the obvious. They analyse rather than describe.

Communication – Take a few minutes to plan the essay. If you rush into your answer it is almost certain you will not make the most of the brief 40 minutes to show all you know about the question. More likely you will include irrelevant details that do not gain you marks but waste your precious time. Remember an essay is formal so do not do the following: story-tell, list and number points, misquote, use slang or colloquial language, be vague, use non sentences or fail to address the question.

HSC STYLE ESSAY QUESTION

Remember that essay responses must respond to essay questions and when you submit a practice essay, it should have a question written at the top. Start by underlining the key words in the question.

The Concept of Discovery may be conveyed differently in and through texts, but the result for responders is a deeper understanding of self and the world.

Discuss this statement with close reference to your prescribed text and two related texts.

PLAN

Introduction Start by introducing the texts you are using in your essay response ***Argument:*** The BOSTES definition for Discuss is to -Identify issues and provide points for and/or against. Consider using differing textual forms which affect how the concept of Discovery is conveyed. For example, a film will convey the concept of Discovery using visual, filmic techniques whereas a novel will use narrative techniques. Using a variety of textual forms will enable you to argue for the first half of the statement and enable you to show the different ways discovery is conveyed. Also consider the rubric and reflect on the different ways Discovery can be and is presented in your texts.	You need to let the marker know what texts you are discussing. You can start with a definition but it can come in the first paragraph of the body. You MUST state your argument in response to the question and the points you will cover as part of it. Don't wait until the end of the response to give it!

Do not forget the second part of the question, that is, the link to you as a responder and your deeper understanding of self and the world, through studying Discovery. You may like to argue that although forms and text types differ and aspects of Discovery raised in and through texts differ, it is this variety which helps you as a responder relate the concept to your own understanding of the world and your place in it.

- (Aim to incorporate discussion of techniques when discussing text and making close textual references.)

↓

Idea 1– Look to the rubric and identify what kinds of Discovery are raised in your texts.

Idea 2- Explore how these are raised, through selected form and relevant techniques.

Idea 3 - Analyse their impact in terms of discovery on you as a responder. Is it a bildungsroman text. Do characters make personal discoveries, grow and learn? Is the composer him or herself a factor linked to a responder and discovery? Look at the purpose in writing the text. Explore these ideas in both your prescribed and related text or texts. In what ways have the aspects of Discovery raised in the three text enhanced your understanding of yourself and the world?

Ideas can be expanded into several paragraphs. be sure to set out paragraphs clearly using a topic sentence, explanation, examples and analysis of examples in terms of technique and link to question.

↓

Finally, your conclusion should incorporate a summary of key ideas. Do not raise new points in a conclusion.

- Provide a final sentence that restates your argument

Make sure your conclusion restates your argument. It does not have to be too long.

DISCOVERY: SUGGESTED RELATED TEXTS

You are often advised to select related texts that do not mirror the form of your Prescribed text. In addition, you are reminded to select related material wisely and look for links to the rubric, the concept and to highlight similarities and differences with prescribed material. Markers have noted that the judicious selection of related material is a key factor when evaluating responses. Sophisticated texts when well analysed in relation to the concept, and strongly analysed in relation to the prescribed text, will impress markers more than texts you may have happened to read at school in previous years in Stage Four or Five.

In the following list, categories are used for convenience but titles are not always exclusive to genre or text type. Many hybrid texts exist which cross boundaries of genre.

PROSE-FICTION/NON FICTION

Bypass – The Story of a Road by Michael McGirr

About one man's journey of discovery along the Hume Highway between Sydney and Melbourne. This is a hybrid text which is part travelogue, memoir, history and romance.

Gulliver's Travels by Jonathan Swift

This classic tale is about Gulliver's discovery of Lilliput. Through his arduous adventures he discovers lessons about society and humanity. The tale is a satirical view of the state of European government, and of petty differences between religions. It addresses the origins of human corruption, the conflict between Lilliputians and Yahoos, and other races.

***A History of Reading* by Alberto Manguel**

Discover a personal response to books and reading and a love of literature. This is a wonderful non-fiction text written by an award winning author.

***Looking for Alibrandi* by Melina Marchetta**

The aspect of discovery here is Alibrandi discovering who her estranged father is, as well as coping with various teenage issues in high school. This text is not as sophisticated as some other choices but it does raise aspects of culture and personal discovery.

***Memoirs of a Geisha* by Arthur Golden**

This novel is about personal discovery and the development of identity in a tumultuous period in Japanese history.

***The Secret River* by Kate Grenville**

Discover the interaction between the white settlers and the Aboriginal population on the Hawkesbury River. The discovery centres on place, people, including the composer, and cultures.

***Small Island* by Andrea Levy**

Told by four narrators, the novel is set during the Second World War and tells the story of four different lives. There is racial tension and discovery of what it is like living with someone who comes from a different part of the world. Not only do you discover this new way of life, but it brings about a discovery of the self.

So Much To Tell You by John Marsden

Here a scarred and introverted girl who is an elective mute, discovers a way to reveal her feelings to the reader in the form of a diary. In turn, readers discover Marina's life and relationships as she also discovers non-verbal ways to communicate with others.

Unpolished Gem by Alice Pung

In this text the Discovery theme involves cultural differences, migration and a new life for an Asian family in Footscray, Victoria. This text is about discovering life in a family and about cultures.

An Unsuitable Job for a Woman by P.D. James

Female detective Cordelia Gray investigates a suicide and a family with many secrets. The writing is detailed with plenty of atmosphere and clues. It is a crime fiction text, detection discovery with a twist. Consider other examples of Crime writing as discovery is a key theme within this genre

The Snowman by Jo Nesbo

Detective discovery in a European setting. This text presents modern take on the genre and is very well written.

FICTION / FILM

***Alice in Wonderland* (novel and film) original by Lewis Carroll**

Alice discovers a magical fantasy world where she is in turmoil. Here she has amazing adventures and meets many intriguing characters.

***Chronicles of Narnia* (novel and film) original by C.S. Lewis**

Four children, Peter, Suzan, Edmund and Lucy, discover a magical world behind their wardrobe and learn about their special role in saving the land from a great evil. The form of allegory can help responders discover deeper truths.

***The Lost Thing* (picture book and film) original by Shaun Tan**

A boy discovers a lost thing and journeys to find it a home.

***The Never-ending Story* (novel and film) original by Michael Ende**

The protagonist Sebastian discovers the world of Fantasia which is dying. He becomes part of the book he is reading and saves the world.

***Sherlock Holmes* (novel and film) original by Conan Doyle**

Any of the *Sherlock Holmes* mysteries of adventures such as *The Hound of the Baskervilles* are recommended. These texts present discovery through means of deduction, calculation and scientific reasoning.

Under the Dome by Stephen King (novel and film)

Imagine being trapped and cut off from the world under a dome of power. This is a Science fiction text that is a long read but an intriguing idea. The initial discovery is awesome but then characters begin to discover things about themselves and others.

Where the Wild Things Are (picture book and film) original by Maurice Sendak

A young boy is punished by his mother to go to his bedroom, which transforms into a jungle where he sails to an island and discovers that it is inhabited by malicious beasts known as the "Wild Things." After successfully intimidating the creatures, Max is hailed as the king of the Wild Things and enjoys a playful romp with his subjects. However, he discovers that being king is not all that great. If you select a Picture book, be sure to discuss visual literary techniques in a sophisticated manner.

Wizard of Oz (novel and film) original by Frank L. Baum

Dorothy discovers a magical fantasy world where various characters discover their true character. For example, Tin Man finds his heart.

The Book Thief by Marcus Zusak

A young orphaned girl meets her new family in Germany during the Second World War. Through the focalisation of this young girl the reader pieces together the narration and discovers what is going on in the world around her. Historical discovery.

FILM

The Island directed by Michael Bay

Science fiction film about clones that live in a false utopian prison who discover their true origins as spare organ parts for wealthy but terminally ill people. The revelation is the discovery and how the discoverers respond to it.

It's Kind of a Funny Story directed by Ryan Fleck

A teenage boy checks himself into the mental ward only to find he has been relocated to the adult's ward. The film follows the boy and the friends he makes along the way.

50/50 directed by Jonathan Levine

Adam learns how to cope and live his life by coming to terms with his cancer.

An Education directed by Lone Sherfig

Jenny is in her final year of high school and has high hopes for the future when she meets a middle aged man who shows her another world. Jenny has to decide which world she wants to live in.

Consider also documentaries and other non fiction filmic forms.

POETRY

A suite of poems rather than one single poem is recommended, especially if the poem is brief.

'Easy Does It' by Bruce Dawe

A poem about discovering his boy and how he has to be 'careful' with him.

'Discovery' by Wislawa Szymborksa

The poem begins with 'I believe in the great discovery' and it is about faith and evidence.

'La Belle Dame Sans Merci' by John Keats

A knight discovers a new love and a new faery world but it is not what it seems and his discovery in this poem leads him to a life of misery.

'My Last Duchess' by Robert Browning

A dramatic monologue which reveals chilling and disturbing details about the speaker.

'Spring and Fall – To a Young Child' by Gerard Manley Hopkins

This is an address to a young girl, Margaret, and raises the discoveries that the child will make about the human condition. There is a prediction that these discoveries concerning life and death will be inevitable and with come with age and maturity.

SONGS

Remember that, if you write about a song, you are advised to consider more than just the lyrics.

At Seventeen by Janis Ian

Teen coming of age song about the angst of discovering what and who you are.

Kings and Queens by 30 Seconds to Mars

Discovering empowerment and greatness from despair.

Meant to Live by Switchfoot

Making the most out of life and discovering your absolute potential.

We Won't get Fooled Again by The Who

The persona in the song discovers that the new government which is established after a revolution is the same as the old government, and criticises it.

WEBSITES

100 Questions to Inspire Self-Discovery

HTTP://WWW.ALEXANDRAFRANZEN.COM/2013/04/18/100-QUESTIONS-TO-INSPIRE-RAPID-SELF-DISCOVERY/

Quite a few sites like this one that offer ideas on the topic. Read judiciously.

Discover the Extreme World

HTTP://WWW.MILESKELLY.NET/PRODUCTS-PAGE/DISCOVERY-EXPLORE-YOUR-WORLD/

Read the book blurb: Produced in association with Discovery Channel, this jam-packed book focuses on the extremes of core reference subjects. From animal giants to futuristic spy technology to the deepest caves and coldest places in the Universe. Nice change as it is aimed at children.

Discover Magazine

HTTP://AU.ZINIO.COM/MAGAZINE/DISCOVER/PR-500621662

Science based but has a wide range of articles on all sorts of interesting topics such as foods and environment.

HTTP://WWW.MILESKELLY.NET/PRODUCTS-PAGE/DISCOVERY-EXPLORE-YOUR-WORLD/

Discovery channel

HTTP://WWW.DISCOVERYCHANNEL.COM.AU/

Here you will discover many shows about discovery but it is also about learning.

Discovery Education

HTTP://WWW.DISCOVERYEDUCATION.COM/TEACHERS/

This address will lead you to the teacher resources but the site is full of content that shows another aspect of discovery i.e. education.

Famous People who Made Scientific Discoveries

HTTP://WWW.BIOGRAPHY.COM/PEOPLE/GROUPS/DISCOVERY/SCIENTIFIC

Another excellent source for evidence in film and written form on a comprehensive site.

Kids Discover

iPad app. Below is the address for the preview but you can download the app and use it. Excellent resource.

HTTPS://ITUNES.APPLE.COM/AU/APP/KIDS-DISCOVER/ID574832964?MT=8

The Science Channel

SCIENCE.DISCOVERY.COM/FAMOUS-SCIENTISTS-DISCOVERIES/100-GREATEST-DISCOVERIES.HTM

Almost complete collection of all the scientific discoveries covering most of the ancient and modern worlds in film and clearly explained.

Self Discovery

HTTP://EN.WIKIPEDIA.ORG/WIKI/JOURNEY_OF_SELF-DISCOVERY

Here are some definitions and links to the topic. A useful starting point to develop your ideas.